Random Journeys - New Zealand

Trevor Cree

Copyright © Trevor Cree 2025

Trevor Cree has asserted his right under The Copyright, Designs and Patents Act 1988 to be identified as the author of this work.

All rights reserved. No part of this publication may be reproduced, stored in a retrieval system or transmitted, in any form or by any means, electronic or mechanical, photocopying, recording or otherwise, without the prior permission of the publisher.

Publisher - Trevor Cree.
Originally published in 2011.
Revised 2025.

ISBN 978-1-0682103-1-0

Introduction

The concept of travelling in a random manner is not new but what if the five, ten or fifty places to be visited have been chosen by drawing letters of the alphabet from a hat to identify the first letters of each location? And then and only then are the actual place names revealed and their location on the map identified. And to add a necessary degree of discipline each and every place must be visited however uninteresting or remote it may seem to be. No convenient substitutions allowed, no deletions, no 'ifs or buts'. A recipe for disaster surely? At least a waste of precious time and precious funds?

Follow Sas and Bro on their 50 day odyssey covering 11,500 km to visit 60 randomly selected locations in New Zealand. And find out what they discovered on their random journey.

Map of Randomly Selected Locations

Each of the randomly selected locations on the map were identified prior to departure from the United Kingdom by drawing letters of the alphabet from a hat to identify the first few letters of each place name and subsequently their geographical location in New Zealand.

The start and finish point for the journey was Napier, Hawkes Bay, and a logical route was devised so that all 60 locations could be covered in the most efficient manner.

The majority of the locations visited would not be on the itinerary of the average traveller and that was what made the experience so unique. In many cases it was a journey into the unknown once the metal road had turned to gravel.

Napier - The journey begins

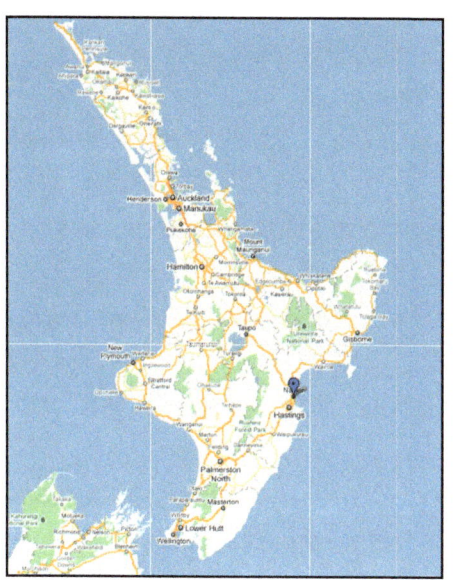

The first time that I saw Sas was on Prebensen Drive. I was on my way to Marine Parade and had only been in the country for three days. She was standing by the side of the road all decked out in pale blue, looking as if she was waiting for someone to take her some place else. I swung a one eighty at the next roundabout and pulled up alongside her for a closer look. She sure was pretty.

'Can I take you for a ride?' I asked.
'Depends where you want to take me but I need to move on from Napier.'
'How about north?'
'But where to?'
'Everywhere.'
'Sounds too vague to me. I need to know exactly where since you're not the only one to have shown an interest.'
'OK then. We would travel all over New Zealand from Houhora in the far north down to Slope Point in the far south.'
'Hou what?'
'Houhora.'
'Never heard of it. I still need to know more if I'm going to head off with a complete stranger.'
'Well here goes. I've been to New Zealand on countless occasions in the past and travelled the country from Cape Reinga in the north to Stewart Island in the south, from East Cape to Hokitika. The Bay of Islands, Coromandel, Abel Tasman, Wanaka, Queenstown, Milford Sound, you name them and I've been there. But this time I decided to do something

different, something a bit unusual, something to take me off the beaten track. Still with me?'

'Just about.'

'Well I had this idea that I would visit sixty places.'

'What's so special about that? People visit hundreds of places on their travels all of the time?'

'True, but they visit or pass through those particular places because they choose to do so.'

'So let me get this straight. You are going to visit places that you don't want to?'

'Exactly. I knew that you would understand. Sorry, I didn't get your name?'

'Sas. The name's Sas. Well it's been good to meet you Bro but actually I'm not that keen on travelling with someone who is planning to visit places that he doesn't want to. Have a good trip.'

'Wait Sas. Wait. I haven't finished my explanation. Of course I want to visit those places. It's just that I didn't choose them.'

'You had a message from God or something? Man you're weird and you definitely need help. Sorry I didn't get your name either?'

'Bro will be just fine. No of course I didn't get a message. I chose the sixty places at random. I drew letters of the alphabet out of the hat to form the first few letters of each place name. And it was only then that I discovered the actual names that matched those letters and where the places were actually located in New Zealand.'

'So why do you want to go to Sleep Point?'

'Slope Point. Because it's there. Because perhaps it's an interesting place. Perhaps no one else goes there. Perhaps it's the most boring place in the world but I will never know unless I actually go there.'

'So why don't you just cut out the places that look boring?'

'You're not taking this seriously are you. Because Sas I believe that every place may have something of interest to offer. And if I omitted places that I didn't like the look of that would defeat the whole point of the random selection. It's the discipline of having to visit all sixty randomly selected locations that makes it worthwhile. It's a journey that

no one else will have ever made before and a journey that no one will ever make in the future.'
'So it's not a guidebook then?'
'Of course it's not a guidebook. You're as bad as the rest of them.'
'Pretty prickly aren't you.'
'Well it's just that nobody understands what I'm trying to do. Look, how many hundred thousand photographs have been taken of Mitre Peak? How many million people have marvelled at Queenstown and Wanaka? I'm not knocking them since they are all incredible places that should not be missed. I'm just trying to stretch the travel experience in a different direction. I want to be taken to places that I haven't chosen to go and force myself to find the hidden secrets and perhaps the heart and soul of each place. I don't want to undertake an in-depth study, just write down my initial impressions of the moment, a personal perspective, sort of sketches of each place, a little background research, perhaps some photographs. Someone else visiting the very same locations as myself may have a completely different take on them. It doesn't matter. And anyone and everyone can do their own random journeys by just selecting five or fifty places to visit in Rome, New York, California, France, Vietnam or wherever. Each journey is then unique, each journey exploring new random places. What do you think?'
'You are definitely mad. When do we start?'
'Sunday.'
'Where to?'
'Gisborne.'

Sas. She sure was pretty.

1. Gisborne

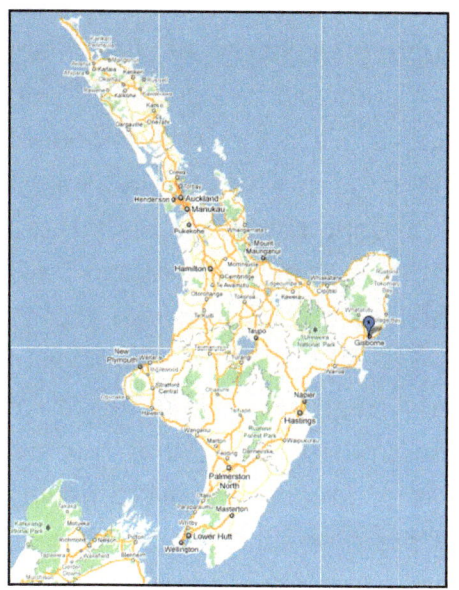

A roll of the dice, a spin of the coin, letters of the alphabet drawn at random from a hat. And there we have Gisborne. Gisborne, a small city but still a city for all that. My heart sank. Where to start? What singular theme could I find to encapsulate such a large place that so much had already been written about?

'So Bro, this is one of those remote places that no one ever visits. Man am I looking forward to this trip.'
'I know Sas. I know. But random is random. We have no choice.'

But then everything slotted into place as if it had been preordained. So obvious really. The very first stop on our journey had by chance directly coincided with the location of the first collision of English and Maori culture. Over 240 years ago, on the 6 October 1769, a young boy standing high in the masthead cried out 'Land!' That boy's name was Nicholas Young, the personal servant of the ship's surgeon William Brougham Monkhouse, and the headland that he saw retains the name 'Young Nick's Head' to this day. We know a great deal about Captain Cook but who was Young Nick? And what became of him? Did he survive the voyage and return to England to lead a full life with a wife, family and descendants? Or did he die young? It seemed such a fruitful line of research but the truth is that virtually nothing is known about the later life and fate of Nicholas Young. The records show that he survived the voyage, no mean feat in that day and age, and later entered the naturalist Joseph Bank's service and accompanied him on his 1772 Icelandic voyage. But after that a complete blank.

So no storyline there but what about a walk to the extremity of Young Nick's Head itself? It seemed so simple and appropriate. To reach the heights and look out to sea in the hope of sighting the imaginary mainsail of the Endeavour, as perhaps a Maori child had done all those years ago, unrecorded. But nothing is simple. Even the most important historical locations are under threat in the world in which we live today. In 2002 there was a public outcry when the land at Young Nick's Head was sold to private owners but fortunately the original 'pa' site and peak of the headland were placed in public ownership. Nevertheless access to the site is through private land and permission from the manager of Nick's Head Station is now required. Even the Department of Conservation seem reluctant for visitors to cross over land that they are currently in the process of conserving and protecting against deeply eroding cliff faces. It is all so sad that a place of such major historical significance to New Zealand is out of bounds to the average Kiwi, and of course, to Sas and I.

The early Maori settlers had previously named Young Nick's Head as 'Te Kuri a Paoa' (the dog of Paoa). Paoa was the captain of the Horouta 'waka' (canoe) on its journey from Hawaiki to New Zealand. Legend has it that Paoa lost his dog in the Poverty Bay area and the dog is still there waiting for his master to return. They say that if you look towards the white cliffs at dawn you may be able to see the outline of Paoa's dog in a crouching position.

In 1906 the Cook Monument was inaugurated with full ceremony in the presence of local and national dignitaries. A photograph of the event illustrates that the monument was well located since it was situated close to the shoreline with clear views across Poverty Bay towards Young Nick's Head. Its position on the northern shore of the Turanganui River marked the actual spot where Cook himself first set foot on New Zealand soil. Mysteriously the photographic record at the site reveals that the monument was originally inscribed with a list of names and other written details. Whether or not this was a list of the original Endeavour crew members could not be ascertained but by 2010 whatever it was that had been inscribed on the monument had been removed and had been carefully replaced by blank pieces of stone. An Orwellian act, the eradication of an inconvenient piece of history? And to heap further humiliation on the site a new wharf had been constructed in the intervening years between the monument and the sea, completely obliterating any view and thus obliterating any meaning. The equivalent of banishing the monument to a parking lot. And up on Titirangi Hill Captain Cook fairs no better in the modern age. His proud form retains the remnants of white paint, one assumes due to the anger of recent protest, whilst the plaque that once existed at his feet has been removed and discarded.

A more recent monument to Captain Cook in Gisborne sits at the end of Customhouse Street making him look like a cross between Tom Thumb and Captain Jack Sparrow. Already the lettering is fading and by the 250th anniversary of the landing the wording will be illegible. It would seem to me that Gisborne, and more importantly New Zealand, has a real problem here to which there is clearly no easy answer.

One solution would be to build a major exhibition hall at the Customhouse Street site to celebrate the arrival of both the original Hourata canoe and Captain Cook, a replica of the canoe with the full story of it's journey and the Maori people who first settled and developed the Poverty Bay area. Proudly celebrating the history of two peoples, one country. Completed by 2019?

'What do you think Sas?'
'Yeah right. Dream on Bro.'

Young Nick's Statue, Gisborne.

Cooks Landing Monument, Gisborne.

Captain Cook Statue, Titirangi Hill, Gisborne.

Captain Cook Statue, Custom House Street.

2. Oponae

So here we were at last, Oponae, our very first no place, nowhere. The road from Gisborne to Opotoki had clearly been a bit of a race track in the past since the level of accidents has persuaded the authorities to construct a number of rest stops along the route in an attempt to reduce the annual carnage. Some hope there. Nevertheless the rest stops are neatly presented with attractive structures made of stone filled caissons in keeping with the slip prone Waioeka Gorge.

Fortunately for us, because it actually had a story to tell, Oponae was selected as one of those rest stops. The origin of the name Oponae derives from the fact that 'ponae' means 'food basket' and 'oponae' means 'your food basket'. So there you have it, clear and simple. Throughout its history 'tuna' (eels), 'inanga' (whitebait) and 'kereru' (pigeon) could be found there. The Waioeka River valley itself had been occupied by the Ngati Ira tribal grouping for hundreds of years and many 'pa' sites had been identified in the past. In the troubled 1860s the Ngati Ira had no choice but to settle close to Oponae at Maraeti Pa under the leadership of Hira Te Popo. This was due to attacks by government troops on a number of 'pa' sites nearer to Opotiki. Oponae's excellent strategic location provided the Ngati Ira with both security and an abundant supply of food during the conflict period. They remained in the area for five years, finally emerging in 1870 to settle at Opeke Marae at the Opotiki entrance to the gorge.

A substantial steel road bridge now crosses the wide but slow flowing Waioeka River at Oponae and a fading wooden signboard proudly declared to all who wished to read it that 'Midway Waioeka could offer the Ultimate Bush Experience', and 'Vacancy', just the encouragement that Sas and I were looking for, evidence of activity. Our detailed map indicated that road access beyond the bridge was actually very limited and so why such an expensive structure should have been built in the first place was a bit of a mystery. The justification may have been to open up the area to farming and forestry as evidenced by the old Tauranga bridge that we had previously visited further down the river. After the earlier upheavals European settlement in the Waioeka Gorge began in earnest in 1880 and intensified in the early 1900s. As settlements grew shops opened up at Matahanea and Oponae and a telephone link was established with the outside world. In the early 1920s even a part-time school was established between Oponae and Wairata. Unfortunately the soil in the area was not fertile enough to maintain sufficient grass growth for stock and over a short space of time much of the land reverted back to bush. Hard won properties were subsequently lost in mortgagee sales whilst others were simply abandoned by their owners. These early settlers had a dream but in hindsight it is clear that this land was not meant to be farmed in the European manner, at least not all those years ago. Perhaps the lesson Oponae has to offer is that, even for the Maori, people will naturally gravitate to the more fertile lowlands and will only try to develop agriculture in remote areas, such as Oponae, in times of extreme stress and necessity.

Driving over the Oponae bridge Sas and I took the right hand road, or more accurately narrow track, and after a short distance our route turned away from the main watercourse to follow a tumbling brown stream inland. It began to look interesting but after barely a kilometre or so the narrow track entered the Oponae Forest and vehicle turning places were notable by their absence. Visions of meeting a fully laden logging truck head-on entered my thoughts, even though no evidence of recent heavy usage could be discerned from the track. I decided that it was just too early in our random travels to get ourselves into a fix, kilometres up a narrow track with nowhere to turn.

'I think that we will have to turn around here Sas. I don't like the look of this track.'
'C'mon Bro, this is exactly what I'm built for. Where's your sense of adventure? Don't be such a wimp. Who knows what we may find around the next corner.'
'Can't risk it I'm afraid Sas. Too early to get ourselves into a fix.'
'Wuss.'
'Sorry?'
'Nothing.'

A few short manoeuvres, carried out between a sheer drop to the stream bed and a steep excavated bank, saw us pointing in the wuss direction. We stopped for a while. So very quiet there, just the gentle sound of flowing water over rock, a tui singing contentedly and a passing rain shower. Perhaps the other route from the bridge might offer us better opportunities, even 'ultimate experiences'. At first the outlook seemed hopeful since the road was much wider and we had noticed that trucks had recently passed in that direction. However after a very short distance that slim hope had also evaporated since the trucks were simply hauling rock and rubble away from what appeared to be a small building site, most probably the previous location of the sadly departed Midway Waioeka. Traveling on past the site the road quickly reverted back into a track and within a very short distance a farm gate barred the way. Beyond the gate the sheep farming potential looked promising but the welcome signs and bunting had not been laid out for visiting strangers. Oponae seemed such a disappointing place for any kind of story. The doubters had been proved right, what was the point in visiting nondescript random places.

But just at that moment we noticed that the route again diverged and a battered old road sign signalled that this was 'Jimmy's Road'. There was no chance to explore Jimmy's Road since the bridge over the stream was too narrow and fragile for a vehicle. In the unknown past a single bullet had deeply dented but not penetrated the letter M on the sign. But who was Jimmy? A hunter, a recluse, a gold prospector or just another dreamer? In the past Jimmy had been someone. Someone whose written legacy still remained for all to see whilst memories of others had long ago faded into history. Let the imagination play with the vision of Jimmy for a moment. Long greying beard, unkempt and matted like his hair, much in need of a good sluicing down. Look at that face, weather beaten and lined, coming on sixty but only forty. Eyes. Penetrating eyes, clear, fixing and worldly wise. They say he was a character by which they meant he was a miserable old sod. A man of very few words, more accurately syllables, a grunt was an achievement. A bent frame he wallowed along but move that rock or fallen tree off the track, he could. Married. Never. Well there was a woman once, when he was young. And then one day, after all those years, Jimmy was gone. Where to no one ever knew.

The answer to the mystery of Jimmy is certainly there to be unraveled but it would just have to wait for someone else. It was for us time to move on. And what about the Oponae 'ultimate bush experience'? The ultimate, it appears, is no longer ultimate. A vacancy is advertised and vacant it will remain.

Bridge over the Waioeka River, Oponae.

Bullet marked Jimmy's Road Sign, Oponae.

3. Rerewhakaaitu

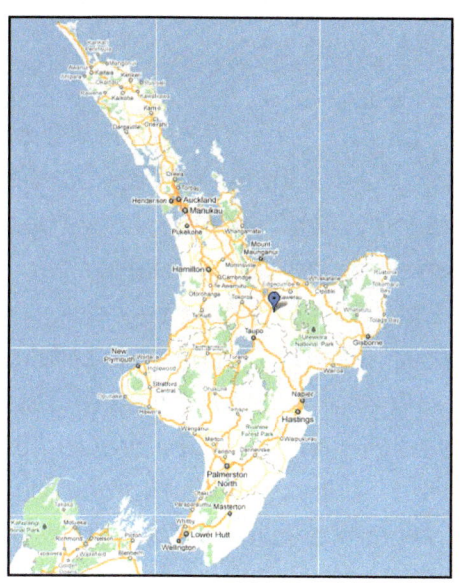

Try pronouncing Rerewhakaaitu after three pints of Guinness.

'Where have you been to Jack?'
'I've just been up to Rerewacktu......Rerefacitu.....Oh sod it, you know, the place with the long name'.

Rerewhakaaitu sits among green rolling hills and close to the lake of the same name. Dairying is the main activity in the area and the early signs of eutrophication of the lake waters, due to animal effluent and fertiliser run-off, is revealed by the initial growth of a red, clogging, suffocating weed close to the shoreline. At present the symptoms are not widespread and the lake is still an enticing stretch of water for bird lovers, campers and fishermen. Rerewakaaitu is a pleasant little settlement with its own school and numerous neat houses stretched along the roadside. Everything seems so peaceful, as it should be on such a minor road.

But first impressions are misleading since every few minutes an empty or fully laden logging truck approaches the single lane bridge at Rerewhakaaitu, the gears change, the air brakes engage and the peace of the place is rudely disturbed. Where the trucks are going to and why is a mystery to the visiting stranger. Even more puzzling is the fact that the fully laden trucks are often going in opposite directions, same loads, same mystery. I'm sure some corporate executive in some far distant capital could explain to Sas and I at length the whole Alice in Wonderland story but to tell the truth we really don't want to know.

But the noise of the trucks is insignificant compared to the event that happened one hundred and twenty four years ago. Close to

Rerewhakaaitu is a rather imposing mountain, its flanks covered in forest. This is Mount Tarawera. The contributor to Wikipedia tells the story so well:

Shortly after midnight on the morning of the 10 June 1886 a series of more than thirty increasingly strong earthquakes were felt in the Rotorua area and an unusual sheet lightening display was observed from the direction of Tarawera. At around 2.00 am a larger earthquake was felt followed by the sound of an explosion. By 2.30 am the three peaks of Mount Tarawera had erupted blasting three distinct columns of smoke and ash thousands of metres into the sky. At around 3.30 am the largest phase of the eruption commenced; vents at Rotomahana obliterated the Pink and White Terraces and produced a pyroclastic surge that destroyed several villages within a six kilometre radius. Although the official contemporary death toll was 153 exhaustive research later identified that 108 people were actually killed by the eruption. Many of the lakes surrounding the mountain had their shapes and areas dramatically altered, including Lake Rerewhakaaitu.

One legend surrounding the 1886 eruption is that of the phantom canoe. Eleven days before the eruption a boat full of tourists returning from the pink and white terraces on Lake Rotomahana saw what appeared to be a war canoe approach their boat, only to disappear in the mist a mile from them. One of the witnesses was a clergyman. Nobody around the lake owned such a war canoe and nothing like it had been seen on the lake for many years. Though skeptics maintained that it was a freak reflection seen on the mist, tribal elders at Te Wairoa claimed that it was a 'waka wairua' (spirit canoe) and was a portent of doom. Locals believe that a future eruption will be signalled by the reappearance of the canoe.'

And so if you ever go to the area be sure to keep a weather eye out for that canoe. Unfortunately you are unlikely to have the opportunity to see what one Rotorua resident described to Sas and I as the 'Ninth Wonder of the World' and that is the seventeen kilometre rift across Mount

Tarawera created by the 1886 eruption. He described it to us as similar to the Grand Canyon but better. On the 1st September 2002 public access to the Mount Tarawera was closed due to 'the vandalism of cars and the desecration of sacred areas'. So all those Maori and 'pakeha' walkers, mountain bikers and tourists are denied access to an amazing scenic experience. That is unless you have money of course. For a reported NZ$ 140 per person a private tour can be arranged using four wheel drive vehicles. So what's happening New Zealand? I can't walk to the end of Young Nick's Head because it is private land and a DOC conservation area. And now I can't see the 'Ninth Wonder of the World'. When you start fencing off sites of national importance to the common man you know that the country is in danger of losing it's way. Let's hope that it is not too late.

Lake Rerewhakaaitu.

Lake Rerewhakaaitu.

Visitors by by Appointment, Mount Tarawera.

Lake Tarawera.

4. Pyes Pa

Pyes Pa is a ribbon settlement with the local school at it's centre. On a clear day there is a fine view down to Tauranga and the imposing Mount Maunganui volcanic outcrop.

The school was first established in 1935 after the previous school at Ngawaro was relocated to where the present Pyes Pa school is situated today. In 1956 the original one room school building was moved back again to Ngawaro to serve as the clubrooms of the Ngawaro Golf Club. The distance between the two locations is seventeen kilometres clearly demonstrating the Kiwi love for moving whole buildings around the country. And so if you look in your rear view mirror and see the Houses of Parliament passing you by on the outside lane of Highway 1 you are neither mistaken nor drunk. Locating the original historic school building in Ngawero seemed a worthwhile objective but on the way from Rotorua to Pyes Pa we had seen no hint of a golf club at Ngawaro, no signpost, nothing. However a few enquiries at the school office revealed that the golf club had actually closed a year or two before but that the location of the old school building could be found directly opposite the Taumata loop road, only half way to Ngawaro. What could be simpler. On our return to that location there was indeed a house nearly opposite the Taumata road and what appeared to be an old building directly behind it hidden by some trees. Approaching the house on foot I was greeted by a particularly aggressive dog and the window of the house opened whereupon the owner shouted a few expletives at the animal and then closed the window again. I concluded that strangers were not that welcome and retreated to have a rethink and possibly abandon the search for the old school classroom.

'Man you should have seen your face when that dog started coming at you. Brave or what.'
'It's OK for you to make fun Sas. I'm the one who has to do all the leg work while you just sit here having a rest.'
'Only kidding Bro.'

It just so happened that at that precise moment an elderly jogger with a clear intent to extend his lifetime beyond infinity passed by on the other side of the road. A few enquiries and he quickly pointed out that the place that we were looking for was a further four hundred metres back in the direction of Pyes Pa, but hidden from the road. Once found the old school was an interesting little building but what the future holds for it is unclear. Perhaps it will be transported back to Pyes Pa school again since it seems to have a love of travel.

Surprisingly for a rural school Pyes Pa is flourishing and the local authorities are actually in the process of adding two more classrooms. The school website reveals the ancient legend of Pyes Pa.

'A long time ago, in the Omanawa district, there used to be a Maori village situated on the cliff tops overlooking a gorge with a flowing river far below. If the village existed today it would probably be in the Taumata Road region. In this village lived a 'puhi', a chief's daughter named Taurikura, who was a woman of high rank. Her village was called Kahakaharoa. Taurikura was very spoiled, she had grown up expecting everything to be done for her. One day Taurikura's grandfather asked her to get him some water from the river. He was far too weak and old to climb down the steep track himself. Taurikura should have obeyed her grandfather but instead she refused to go, telling her 'koro' she was too tired. Her grandfather was very thirsty, so, in desperation he decided to fetch the water himself. He climbed down the steep track to the river carrying his empty gourd. Eventually he reached the river and was able to quench his thirst. He then filled his gourd and carried it back up to the 'pa'. Taurikura, seeing that her grandfather had water in his gourd when he returned to the 'pa', demanded that she be allowed it for herself. Her

grandfather, unable to believe how cheeky his 'mokopuna' was, became angry with her, telling her that she was selfish and that he was very disappointed in her. Turning his back on his granddaughter he returned to his 'whare'. Taurikua was filled with embarrassment and shame, she knew she had behaved badly towards her grandfather. Feeling that she could no longer face her tribe she left the village carrying a kit of charms with her. Later that night she crept down to the river and changed herself into a 'ngarara', a creature resembling a lizard. She swam downstream towards Tauranga Moana, past the estuary of Waikareao, on past Matarawa (the old name for Judea), past Motupae and out into Tauranga Moana. She swam on past the mountain known as Mauao, beyond Matakana, stopping finally, exhausted, on the rocky island of Karewa. Keeping her lizard form so that no one would ever recognise her, Taurikura stayed on Karewa where she became the ancestor of the tuatara, a special type of lizard who share their nests with mutton birds, found only on Karewa. Taurikura is especially remembered at Judea where she can be seen in the carved 'poupou' at the meeting house Tamateapokaiwhenua. There is a carved portrait of Taurikura, the cheeky girl, who is the ancestor of the tuatara of Karewa.'

And so there you have it. Behave yourself Sas and Bro at the back of the class. Respect your elders, pay attention and sit up straight.

'Gee Bro, that teacher sure is a hard case.'
'Sure is Sas. I think that I prefer the dog.'

The Legend of Taurikura, Pyes Pa.

Old Pyes Pa School, Ngawaro.

View from Pyes Pa towards Mount Maunganui.

5. Gordon

Gordon sits below the towering forested escarpment of the Kaimai Range of mountains which separate the Waikato from the Bay of Plenty. A little way south of the settlement the waters of the Wairere Falls leap into space demonstrating the extensiveness of the back country catchment area. And still nearer Gordon a railway tunnel, eight kilometres in length and therefore worthy of mention, had years before been bored and blasted through the mountain to transport goods from the port of Tauranga to various destinations within New Zealand.

There is certainly a peaceful air about Gordon and neighbour sits some distance from neighbour, close enough to assist, far enough not to intrude. It is typical dairying country and the Waihou river ambles past on its way north to the Firth of Thames. As early as 1897 a creamery was established in Gordon powered by a four horsepower stationary steam engine. Every morning the farmers would arrive with their horse and carts and urns of milk to be processed, after which the cream would then be transported onwards to a butter factory at Ngaruawahia. The creamery closed in 1920.

The wonders of digital imaging allow an internet user in a far off country to explore the Gordon area in great detail but the resultant emotion is flat and lifeless, and can never capture the scent of the grass, daisy and clover, the sound of the skylark or the coolness of the early summer air. But Gordon has not always been so peaceful. On the 3rd July 1963 a Douglas DC-3 Skyliner of the National Airways Corporation crashed in the Kaimai Range with the loss of three flight crew and twenty passengers. At the time it was the worst aviation accident in New

Zealand history and a monument on the Old Te Aroha road poignantly marks the event. The menfolk of Gordon were foremost in the search for the plane due to their intimate knowledge of the area.

The Kaimai Mamaku Forest Park adjacent to Gordon covers 37,000 hectares and is said to be a living museum of natural and human history. The park marks the northern limit of kamahi, red and silver beech, and the southern limit of the huge kauri, a climatic boundary between the north and south of the nation. In 1881 a prospector, Hone Werahiko, found gold in the Waiorongomei Valley, just north of Gordon. By 1884 between three and four thousand people were living in Waiorongomai township but the gold mines were never very successful due to the cost of extracting the ore from the unexpectedly hard rock. However the Piako County Tramway, built in 1882-83, remains New Zealand's most intact example of a mining tramway. It was used to shift carts of ore and consisted of three distinct self-acting inclines, of which the Butlers Incline is four hundred metres in length. Over a period of six years work was carried out by the Department of Conservation to upgrade the walking tracks and to restore the tramway and this project was finally completed in 2009. The walk to the head of the Butler Incline takes an hour of steep climbing but it is certainly well worth the effort.

On the way I passed a beautiful little waterfall and I am sure that Hone Werahiko was there to watch over the path. Look at the waterfall photograph carefully. Can you see the mouth first, above it the nose and the cheek, then the eye and forehead? Remember, look after the forest because Hone is watching.

Memorial to Air Crash Victims, Gordon.

Kaimai Range Landscape, Gordon.

Hone Werahiko is watching you, near Gordon.

View from the track to Butlers Incline, near Gordon.

6. Otway

So you think that Holland is flat? Welcome to Otway. The only way that you can determine that you have actually arrived at the correct location is that the map shows that Otway is to be found at a road junction and that road fortunately happens to be named Otway Road.

The name Otway actually commemorates a pioneering family whose best known representative in recent times was a Mr L Seton Otway. He was both a farmer and a breeder of thoroughbred horses and it was he who made the Trelawney Stud in Cambridge famous throughout the racing world. No settlement at all is to be found at Otway, just one or two scattered houses in acres of pasture. When you draw letters from a hat at random you hope that you will obtain an even spread of places throughout the whole country, a representative selection. But that is not what random gives you, is it. Random is random and so once again I stand in yet another flourishing dairying area and just a short distance from my next port of call, Springdale, also in the same flourishing dairying area. But after all this is New Zealand, the home of the butter and cheese that I grew up on. In fact I nearly own the place.

Otway is actually not at all unpleasant. It's another beautiful sunny day and the birds are singing to their hearts content. A farmer with his vintage Massey Ferguson tractor and equally antique mower prepares to cut a rather sparse looking field of grass to make hay for winter feed. There is no doubt that this is a rich farming area as far as the vagaries of the world commodity markets allow. Milk production, king one year, pauper the next. I sense that it just can't feel the same way that it used to in Otway for the men and women who actually farm this land. Now large corporations in far off capitals speculate in land as a productive unit, where the actual workers are just costs of production in a financial director's spreadsheet, to be deleted with the single press of a computer key. No wonder farmer suicide rates around the world are so high.

'Well this place is a bunch of fun Bro. It must be in the top ten places to see before you die.'
'Very amusing Sas. Your talents have been completely wasted. Look, this is what this journey is all about. We just have to take what we have been given or just pack up and go home.'
'You mean that it would be back to that secondhand car lot on Prebensen Drive? Now hold on. There's a lot to be said for this place. Just breath in that air, feel the sun on your back, listen to the birdsong. It kinda grows on you.'
'I knew that you would come round to my point of view Sas.'
'One hundred percent Bro. One hundred percent.'

For a brief moment I feel that I am Cary Grant in the film North by Northwest, standing by the side of a straight road that stretches into infinity in both directions. I am at the appointed place to meet someone but nobody comes. And then, in the far distance, I see an old biplane dusting maize, it turns towards me and flies low with a clear intent to kill. I dive to the ground and then flee into the tall enveloping maize crop. But there is no plane, no threat, no maize. Just Otway.

'Hey Bro, come out of the sun. It has a strange effect on some people. Is that boy crazy or what?'

The Otway Road, Otway.

Bottles of an ancient vintage, Otway.

Landscape, Otway.

7. Springdale

Originally the Springdale area was a rather desolate swamp which formed part of the more widely known Piako Swamp. In the late nineteenth century it was owned by land development companies but their efforts to farm there did not prove successful. Subsequently most of the area was subdivided into smaller farm sections and allocated to individual farmers. The tasks of these early settlers was clearly unenviable. They set out to break in their land with their bare hands and horses only to find that the tree stumps that they had removed had been sitting on another layer of tree stumps below, and in many cases even a third layer below that. It is only by understanding the original state of the land that Sas and I can fully appreciate the 'sweat and tears' that went into making the area what it is today. And many of those that farm in Springdale today are descendants of those early settlers.

It seems as if the Springdale area is still awaiting the Japanese invasion in World War II since the No 1 Road leads to the No 9 Road and then on to the No 6. The road numbering system is reportedly based on the numbers of the adjacent drainage channels but Sas and I know that it is just a ruse to confuse the enemy and indeed visiting strangers, such as ourselves. However we found Springdale with little difficulty and this time a small community actually existed. There is a school, community hall, ancient petrol station and a pretty little white walled and red roofed church building. The former church is now The Old Church Gallery offering 'unique accommodation' and in a typical Kiwi manner gallery hours are 'By Appointment (or chance)'. And all about Springdale are fields of pasture in every direction.

I pulled into the Springdale petrol station to fill up since it seemed appropriate to inject a little capital into the area. The lady who served me said that she had been born on one of the local farms but indicated that they were not as productive as they used to be. She seemed to imply that it was a case of ownership by large corporations again, but I really don't know.

A car and a boat were in the adjacent workshop for servicing but it was apparent that the business would struggle to keep going long into the future. Like so many small rural communities the farms get larger, the population gets smaller, the school roll less, the business opportunities fewer and before long you have depopulated areas. A few local advertisements and personal notices adorned the petrol station window. One notice particularly caught my eye and it consisted of a photograph of a young man in a cowboy hat and above the photo was typed in large letters,

'Work Wanted - Barn Building. I will build your barn in a day. Payment in kind or 10 flagons of cider vinegar or use of a sturdy horse'.

Naturally I thought that it was for real, even if it was a little odd. I mentioned this to the lady behind the counter and she said that it was actually a joke on the man, perhaps to bring him down a peg or two. It had been in the window for three weeks and he had yet to see it. His reaction when he finally saw it would no doubt be a picture to see. And so life still continues within the community. After Springdale I decided to return along my original route to Otway in order to take one or two more photographs. But this time I mixed up my No 1 Road with my No 7 Road with my No 4 Road and got briefly lost. Bloody Japs.

'Go easy on the Jap bit Bro. I've got feelings too you know.'
'Sorry Sas. I forgot where you originally came from. You've got such a neat Kiwi accent now.'
'Yeah, well just remember the next time.'

Springdale Service Station.

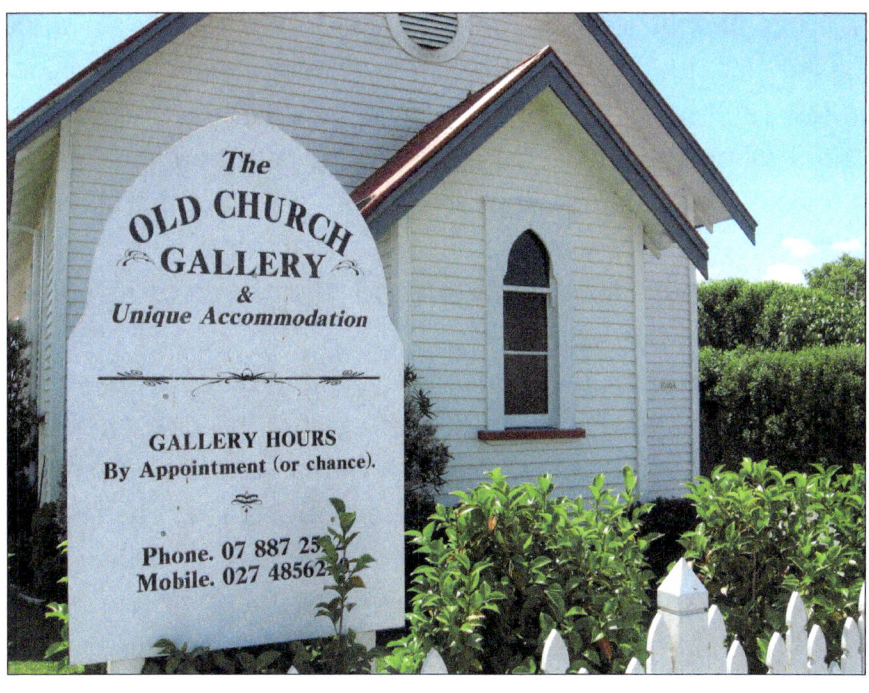

By Appointment (or chance), The Old Church Gallery, Springdale.

8. Algies Bay

Alexander Algie and his brother Samuel migrated to New Zealand from Glasgow in the 1860s and worked in the Pakiri bush for some years. Samuel Algie subsequently married Elizabeth Skeates of Auckland and settled at Martins Bay. His brother Alexander bought a property at a location close to Martins Bay that has ever since been known as Algies Bay. He settled there in 1867 with his wife, Mina Deerness, who had come to New Zealand with her parents from the Orkney Islands. Alexander's father later lived with the family at Algies Bay so that by 1977 there had been five generations of the family living at that location. In May 1877 Alexander was appointed postmaster for the Mullet Point district. He kept that office until December 1923 when his son John took over and he stayed in charge until 1949 when the office was closed, thereby ending a continuous period of service by father and son of 72 years. A brief search of the local telephone directory indicated that there were currently no Algie families living in the district but their name clearly lives on in Algies Bay.

There is no doubt that the location is a small piece of paradise. The historic Kawau Island acts as a barrier against the direct power of the not so pacific sea and provides the area with an expansive yet safe area for race sailing. To the south lies a green headland, pasture now but which no doubt has property developers salivating over their pinot noir and waking up in the middle of the night fearful that their competitors have got there first. Perhaps some far off multi-billionaire has already bought the lot. Who knows?

A snowstorm of white sails suddenly blows onto the Algies Bay slipway with tiny terrors everywhere and not so tiny parents eagerly helping their proto-champs to pull their dinghies out of the water. Bisto, Blondie, Super Star, The Fiddler, Lorenzo and many other pet names race up the slipway and home, home, to ice cream and supper.

I walk along the beach and come across a stone bench with an attractive carving of a horse on the back. Somebody cared enough to share the view with others. Stretching down to the shoreline beautiful homes sit in their magnificence and so far public access has not been prohibited. There is a pleasant feel about the place, relaxed and welcoming. You certainly have to be rich to live in Algies Bay but you don't have to be rich to sail or spend some time there. A warm breeze blows onshore, the sun shines and its time to leave.

'So that's it then Bro?'
'Well yes, what else?'
'The road to Mahurangi of course.'
'But what's at Mahurangi Sas?'
'I don't know do I. But it's worth a look.'
'But it's a road to nowhere and we will then have to retrace our tracks.'
'Exactly. A road to nowhere. That's what we're doing isn't it? Searching for the unexpected, that's what you said.'
'But we've already visited the place that we were meant to.'
'We got lost. Inadvertently departed Algies Bay in the wrong direction'.
'I don't believe it. OK then.'

There is something attractive about travelling towards the end of a narrow peninsula with no exit. The drive was certainly worth the effort with glimpses of beautiful views both inland and out to sea. The blight of a huge padlocked steel gate with a sign shouting, 'Private Property: No Access', temporarily subdued the mood but it was soon passed by. Towards the end the road turned to gravel and Sas was in her element. And then we were there. Mahurangi.

'It's just beautiful young Sas. Absolutely beautiful.'
'Less of the young. I'm fifteen.'

It was certainly peaceful that afternoon. A small wharf provided moorings for one or two boats and close by stood the historic Scott Homestead. Thomas Scott junior built the Georgian style house in 1877 on the site where his father, a shipbuilder, ran an inn until it was destroyed by fire. Although not open to the public the building gave a sense of what it must have been like to have lived in Mahurangi all those years ago.

'Home then Sas?'
'And?'
'Well thanks for insisting that we came here.'
'You're welcome.'

A Snowstorm of Sails, Algies Bay.

Sailing Course Marshalls, Algies Bay.

Bench with Horse Sculpture, Algies Bay.

The Scott Homestead, Mahurangi.

9. Ti Point

In 1886 the land that comprised the Dacre's Claim area was surveyed and since Ti Point was unoccupied at the time it was also included in the survey. The surveyed land was subsequently offered for sale at £1 an acre, the purchaser having the choice of a cash purchase or a ninety nine year lease. An advance in cash for clearing the land and a number of fruit trees was also included in the sale price.

One of the would-be purchasers of a section at either Dacre's Claim or Ti Point was a young man who walked all the way from Auckland to view the land open to ballot. That man was William Torkington, a builder, who successfully secured a section of land and also found plenty of building work in the district. One of the few remaining structures built by William Torkington, a beautiful church, can be seen at the Matakana Country Park. Having been moved from its original site it now looks out of place, stranded as it is in a theme park, lonely and abandoned by it's congregation.

The first names on the Ti Point school list were recorded in 1895 and it is believed that at that time it was a part-time school sharing its teacher with the Dacre's Claim school. The school was erected on an acre of land bounded on two sides by a road and on another by a tall Ti tree. The Ti tree is more commonly known as manuka which, apart from its global reputation for honey production, is also a favourite firewood because of its distinctive aroma whilst also burning extremely well.

A 1922 photograph of the pupils identifies four Torkington children, no doubt descendants of the original William Torkington or his close relatives. At the time a number of the children rode to school and so there was always land available for a horse paddock. It must have been a wonderfully leisurely journey so different from the rushed 'mother's late for work' four-wheel drive shuttle of today. The last teacher arrived at Ti Point school in 1936 and his name was Cliff Brooking. He later recalled that: '

Not only was the scenery most spectacular but the people were most friendly and helpful. I was shocked to find that many of the pupils could not swim and so, whenever the tide was right and the weather suitable, I used to take swimming lessons just below the school on the beach near the old public works quarry. I was surprised to find that only three Maoris attended the school, they were children from the Brown family - Buster, Tui and Inez.'

The Reptile Park at Ti Point is New Zealand's only zoo specialising in reptiles and currently breeds both New Zealand and exotic species. I did not know beforehand but for an animal to be classified as a reptile it must have scales, be cold blooded and obtain its oxygen from the air. Furthermore reptiles are classified into four orders, Crocodilia (crocodiles and alligators), Sqaumata (lizards and snakes), Chelonia (tortoises and turtles) and Rhynchocephalia (tuataras).

'Have you got that Sas?'

'Not really interested.'

Close by to the reptile park lies the Ti Point vineyard which is unusually managed by three female generations of the same Haslam family, daughter, mother and grandmother. The gravel road to the end of Ti Point suddenly seemed so familiar and it was only then that I realised that I had been there before, exactly when I could not say but I believe it was 2004. The antique Judith Aimee lies serenely at anchor, as she has done for decades, arctic tern dive vertically into the water seeking fish and making one jump with their unexpected *thurruumph* as they break through the surface. Huge boulders line the shore as if positioned by man for artistic effect.

Young fishermen cast their lines knowing that their catch is limited to nine snapper, enough to feed a tribe. The warm evening air envelopes as the waves wash against the sand. I meet two fishermen, Chinese it seems, on my return.

'Good fishing?' I ask.

'No', one replies.

'Can I have a look?'

'No'.

I guess nine snapper is generous but not enough for some.

Rock Formation, Ti Point.

William Torkington's Church, Matakana Country Park.

10. Langs Beach

It's all very strange because I know that I have visited Langs Beach more than once in the past but it feels completely new to me. The beach is deserted and the Hen and Chicken islands look so dramatic, as if they are acting as a backdrop for the movie South Pacific. I walk along the beach to the southern end. A single boat, small in size, heads swiftly towards the shore and the two fishermen back a tractor and trailer into the water, load their boat and head off home with their morning catch. A number of cormorants sit on rocks just out of harms way, spreading their wings and warming themselves in the sun.

Unfortunately all is not so peaceful at Langs Beach since the nearby Te Arai Beach is in danger of becoming the next coastal development site if the property developers get their way. Plans for 850 houses, a hotel, shops, tennis courts, swimming pools, health spa, conference centre and golf course have already been submitted to the district council for approval. There are literally hundreds of unsold properties for sale within forty five minutes of the beach and yet still the developers want more. Local people are angry and there are a number of reasons against the development. For example, the area is home to eight native birds, five of which are endangered, and one of the birds nesting in the area is the New Zealand fairy tern which is New Zealand's rarest bird. In fact there are only 35-40 fairy tern left in the whole of the country. The experts feel that further extensive development in the area will likely lead to their extinction and deal a fatal blow to yet another piece of New Zealand's native wildlife. Additional native breeding birds include the northern NZ dotterel, oyster catcher, pied stilts, banded dotterel, spur winged plover, caspian tern, and the white fronted tern. Somehow it seems that every square inch of New Zealand is up for sale to the highest bidder, wherever they happen to come from, as long as they can pay the price. It's a global addiction and everyone who has property or land is involved because for many it's the only source of wealth that they have left. And the classic Joni Mitchell words comes to mind *'Don't it always seem to go that you don't know what you've got till it's gone, they paved paradise and put up a parking lot.'* It's all so sad.

At the southern end of Langs Beach lies millionaires row with spectacular views all the way up to Bream Head. John and Irene walk along the beach every morning. It's what they promised themselves when they had the new place built to replace the old bach that had been in the family for years. They had hoped that their children and grandchildren would visit regularly once they had retired to Langs Beach since the voluminous space was so empty without the laughter of children. But the pressures of city life meant that their loved ones rarely came to visit. It seemed so different from the original bach which had no fresh water, flushing toilet, electricity or other conveniences but then it had always seemed so glorious. In those days they had made love long and often. In the late evening they now sat apart in what was rapidly becoming a mausoleum, a virtual mortuary for the as yet undead.

'Give it a rest Bro'.
'Give what a rest Sas?'
'This housing development business. It's becoming a bit repetitive, a bit of a bore.'
'But it's important Sas. You know that'.
'I know Bro but if you carry on like this you will lose all your readers. I think they get your drift by now.'
'OK Sas. Not another word. I promise. But'.
'No buts Bro or you'll be walking.'
'I get the picture'.

View to Hen and Chicken Islands, Langs Beach.

Our little place by the sea, Langs Beach.

11. Nukutawhiti

The Ngapuhi ancestor Nukutawhiti was the captain of one of the legendary canoes that originally settled New Zealand, namely the Ngatokimatawhaorua canoe. And so to have your settlement named after Nukutawhiti is certainly something to be proud of but how, why and when it received that name I do not know. The Ngapuhi are the largest Maori tribe in New Zealand and their heartland lies at Te Tai Tokerau in the far north, whilst their territory stretches from Hokianga Harbour to the Bay of Islands, and southward to Maunganui Bluff and Whangarei. The tribe's founding ancestor, Rahiri, was descended from Kupe, Nukutawhiti and Puhi. When his two sons fought over land Rahiri helped them make peace by flying a kite over the area and the points where it landed marked the boundary between their two regions of influence, namely Hokianga and Taumarere.

I had not anticipated seeing anything of note whilst driving from Whangarei to Kaikohe, the road on which Nukutawhiti sits, but I have now unofficially renamed it as the 'Serene Highway'. The road runs parallel to the two main north-south highways and yielded up open vistas to distant hills and a very pleasant and relaxed driving experience. At first I thought that I might have missed Nukutawhiti since many of the settlements that I had passed on the way did not have the formality of a signpost to identify them. However I remembered from my research, undertaken many weeks before, that there should be a pretty little church on my left hand side and suddenly there it was, just as I remembered it. A small stone memorial directly adjacent to the main entrance, with its lettering rapidly fading, read as follows,

'All Saints Church. In living memory this church was erected by the late Arona brothers of Mangakahia as a memorial tribute to their forebears who were closely associated with the early missionaries under the late Bishop Patterson of Melanesia. Dedicated by the late Bishop Bennett of Aotearoa as a centre of worship for the people and descendants on May 13th 1934. How the Mighty are Fallen'.

It was therefore particularly poignant to read a recent entry in the visitors book made by Deacon Arona, Aidan Arona and Michelle Arona, all of Sydney. One can only assume that this was a personal pilgrimage to Nukutawhiti by the descendants of the Arona brothers who were mentioned in the inscription.

In many ways our visit to Nukutawhiti seemed to be about the historical importance of religious faith and how it has faded in just one or two generations. And, as if to emphasise the point, just inside the entrance is a photograph of three men standing outside of the church and written below is, almost desperately:

'Yes, we are small. And there are those who would get rid of these little churches. Nevertheless, where two or three are gathered together in my name, there am I in the midst of them.' And I say 'Amen' to that.

We drove onwards to Twin Bridges where the Mangakahia River joins another river flowing from the north. The river is full of trout each contentedly holding their station against the flow. Under the trees bags of refuse have been discarded but whether by local youngsters having a party, or by freedom campers, it is impossible to tell. The concept of freedom camping is wonderful but it seems that it is commonly abused, particularly by certain visitors from abroad. The problem arises from the fact that many hired camper vans do not have toilet facilities leading to the obvious outcome. The only way to combat the problem is to ensure that every hire van has a toilet of some kind but people who should know better will still continue to abuse the environment and the people who live there. As Roger Waters once sang, *'the human race has amused itself to death.'*

All Saints Church, Nukutawhiti.

A Testament to Faith, Nukutawhiti.

The Graveyard, Nukutawhiti.

12. Merita

When I mentioned the name Merita to the owners of the backpacker hostel where I stayed the night neither of them had ever heard of the place even though they knew the Karikari Peninsula well and the wife's ancestors had lived in the area for generations.

And when I went searching for Merita myself, detailed map in hand, I totally missed the place and carried on to Maitai Bay completely oblivious to my mistake until the road came to an abrupt end at the beach. But Maitai Bay is indeed an exceptional location and so many times during our travels we have chanced upon sights of similar unexpected beauty. And at this time of the week and year, namely midweek and a few weeks before Christmas, the Maitai beach and camping grounds were virtually deserted. Seven or eight simple holiday bachs sit high above the bay, as they have done for years, like gold prospectors who have staked their claim. The children and grandchildren of the original owners hope and pray that one day, when the rules change, they can make their fortune and by doing so lose the very thing that their forbears valued so much, the simplicity and the view.

After a short time at the beach we drove back along the road in search of Merita and turned left along the gravel Wairahoraho Road but no signpost marked the Merita settlement or indicated its existence, even though I instinctively knew that we had arrived. There were no views to the sea and so no one was knocking on doors to make offers that the owners could not refuse, just yet. A small traditional red roofed church sat proudly on the hill overlooking the area but somehow I suspected that it may have already been converted into a home.

Many years ago, in 1946, the Anglican Primate of New Zealand came to dedicate the church. At that time a very close-knit community of about twenty Maori families lived in the area and very few 'pakeha' knew the place because access was limited to a beach road or by boat. On the 1st of May 1946, when the ceremony was due to take place, a tremendous storm came and waves broke high over the beach right up to the sand dunes. The next day, Simon Urlich, a black-bearded giant directly descended from Hiione drove his truck to the end of the beach to pick up the Primate and his entourage. The waves were still breaking around the truck as it made its way along the beach but the journey was successfully completed and the church was consecrated. It had been no easy task to build this church on the hill. Over a period of forty years money had been slowly accumulated and held in trust by members of the Reihana family. Then finally, in 1946, under the direction of Ruki Stevens and with labour given freely by local people the church began to take shape. It was constructed in the conventional style with native timbers and a very large mat, woven in sections by the women of the community, completely covered the sanctuary. And so that is how the church on the hill came to be.

The surrounding Merita landscape consisted of a few beehives, grazing beef cattle, skylarks singing their warning cry, and when a single car passed by throwing up gravel and dust we moved on. A little further back down the road there is the sadness that is the Carrington Golf Estate with its 'private property' and 'security' notices littering the boundary fence line to keep out the 'whanau' and the common man. I felt so strongly about the keep out signs but it had nothing to do with envy. The views across the Carrington estate to the white sand dunes beyond were certainly fine but the golf course itself wasn't particularly special. It's the pseudo exclusiveness of the place that annoyed me. You just feel that the owners would have thrown Michael Campbell off if he happened to skip over the fence to practice a few shots. Perhaps the estate provides a small amount of local employment in the hotel, vineyard and caddy shack but you sensed that the caddies would still occasionally be referred to in a denigrating way by some geriatric millionaire or third world despot. There is no way that the golf course could be financially viable to own except to help offset the corporate tax bill in the Cayman Islands. When will it all end?

'So I guess that you don't play golf Bro?'
'Yes I do Sas. I play off 20.'
'As I said, you don't play golf.'
'Very droll Sas. Very droll.'

A Carrington Golf Estate Welcome, near Merita.

Mangonui, on the road to Merita.

The Church on the Hill, Merita.

Bee Hives and Beef Cattle Farming, Merita.

13. Houhora

The heart of Houhora is in a superb location adjacent to an extensive tidal inlet. Various wading birds, none that I could name, seemed to love the place. The Houhora Tavern is set a little way back from the main Kaitaia to Cape Reinga road and was hidden from view by tall pine trees so that most drivers would pass Houhora without even noticing it. The pub interior is a throwback to the typical Kiwi tavern of so many years ago and it is easy to conjure up visions of jugs of beer, the Friday night swill and fights over nothing in the gravel road outside. A notice at the doorway declared that 'No drugs to be consumed on the premises' and I can picture the local lads saying 'We're in the garden Marlene, look after the kids'. The landlord had been trying for eight years to get a proper surface for the gravel road outside of the tavern because the uncontrolled slides of the hoons and the subsequent dust was no good for business. But today was indeed the day and at midday precisely the council contractors arrived with a grader, road roller and a mob of men. And they got stuck in with barely a glance at the watering hole, so tempting and so close by. An elderly couple, with their personal snooker cues in hand, contentedly peered out of the window of the tavern to watch the free entertainment.

Adjacent to the tavern the Houhora Shop and Information Centre was at your service to meet your every need except that it didn't look as if it had been open for years. Alongside was the Old Houhora Post Office but no stamps would be sold today or any other day, no letters posted to relatives in Kerikeri, no local gossip exchanged. At one time they were clearly attractive buildings but that is what happens to dying communities when trade passes them by. And yet perhaps today is the new beginning, a few pine trees accidentally cut down to reveal the tavern to passers-by, the road renovations finalised, the homemade beef burgers with meat that truly tasted like meat, the landlord with a bagful of character and energy, not forgetting his wife, and a permanent main road diversion past the pub and all will be well. Houhora will indeed live again.

I clearly missed something important during my visit because Houhora is actually a place of historic and environmental significance. On our road journey north we never saw a single indication that this was so, no banners, no signboards, absolutely nothing. In fact Houhora mountain was the first land mass of New Zealand that the early Maori explorer Kupe sighted and according to the legend he thought it was a whale. Houhora subsequently became a major Maori settlement as early as the 14th century and in total 3,200 archaeological objects are known from the site. These items included adzes, ornaments, fishing gear, bone harpoon points, bone needles, tattoo chisels, bone chisels and awls and manufacturing tools such as stone drill points, hammer stones, sandstone files and scrapers. These people from the early fourteenth century were already following a seasonal round of food procuring, preservation and storage which persisted for hundreds of years.

On the 10th December 1769, Captain James Cook named the Houhora mountain Mount Camel and described it in his ship's log as 'a high mountain or hill standing upon a desert shore'. In the 19th century Houhora harbour provisioned whalers and residents mounted their own whaling expeditions in open boats. A lifeboat from the ship named 'Elingamite', which was wrecked on the distant Three Kings Islands on the 9th November 1902, arrived in Houhora on the following day with 52 survivors. The harbour has recently been designated as a site of international significance as a result of habitats used by international migratory wading birds, including the turnstone, knot and godwit, whilst other birds of importance are the New Zealand dotterel, reef heron, bittern, banded dotterel, wrybill and black stilt. And so there is so much that Houhora has to offer to the thousands of local and foreign visitors who travel the road to Cape Reinga every year. If any place deserves support in New Zealand then it is historic Houhora.

The Houhora Tavern.

Houhora Inlet.

The Old Houhora Shop and Information Centre, Houhora.

14. Omapere

What strikes you most about Hokianga Harbour, apart from it being another wonder of the world, is the peace of the place. Some people seem to get washed up there by the ocean breakers and never move on. It was the case for the first Maori navigator Kupe and it was the same for Travis, 'The Sage of Omapere'. I would guess that Travis must be in his sixties, or even seventies, and he spends half the year in the north of England where he was born and the other half in New Zealand. Originally he worked as a merchant seaman and that is how he first came to know the country. In the past he used to travel around visiting all the major scenic attractions until a few years ago he decided that Omapere suited him just fine and there he would stay. It seems that what keeps him happy is a simple cup of tea and a chat. And there are plenty of people to talk to since there is a continuous stream of backpackers from all corners of the world eager to share their experiences. New Zealand is no longer inexpensive and they are moving quickly but Travis just stays put. He has no need to move on since every day there are new people to talk to, each with their different stories. One day Travis will move on, or will be moved on, but for the time being if you want a leisurely chat just call in on Omapere.

Directly opposite the settlement lies the entrance to Hokianga Harbour where the changing tide and wind can whip the sea up into a blue and white frenzy. The original Maori names for the area are 'Te Kohanga o Te Tai Tokerau' which means 'the nest of the northern people' and 'Te Puna o Te Ao Marama' which means 'the wellspring of moonlight', the latter pure poetry. The full name of the harbour is 'Te Hokianga-nui-a-

Kupe', namely 'the place of Kupe's great return'. The Maori certainly had a beautiful descriptive way with words. According to Te Tai Tokerau tradition, Kupe, the legendary Polynesian navigator and explorer, settled in Hokianga in approximately 925 AD after his journey of discovery from Hawaiiki aboard the waka (canoe) named Matahorua. When he left Hokianga he declared that this would be the place of his return. Later Kupe's grandson Nukutawhiti returned from Hawaiiki to settle in Hokianga.

The first European ship to enter Hokianga Harbour was the Providence captained by Captain Herd in 1822. The forests in the area were extensive and his ship was the first to sail with a shipment of timber, a trade that would last until the early 1900s when little commercial timber remained. In 1837 a French aristocrat with delusions of grandeur, Baron Charles de Thierry, sailed with 60 settlers into this hive of export activity to claim an immense tract of land that he believed he had purchased for 36 axes, fifteen years earlier. He was eventually granted about 1,000 acres at Rangiahua where he set up his colony declaring himself 'Sovereign Chief of New Zealand', a title that failed to endear him to the Ngapuhi tribe and in the end his settlement collapsed.

The sand hills which form the northern entrance to the harbour are a truly amazing sight. How the sand hasn't been washed or blown away over the millennia is difficult to understand. It's as if someone in Disneyworld had decided that they wanted to make the harbour entrance even more spectacular and simply decided that they would transport a billion tons of sand to the place for scenic effect.

View towards Hokianga Harbour and dunes, Omapere.

Globetrotter Backpacker, Omapere.

15. Poutu

It was at times like this on my random odyssey that I felt that I was the luckiest person in the world. Indeed, I was the luckiest person in the world. The journey to Poutu was a journey to nowhere since after sixty seven kilometres there was only one option and that was to return in the same direction that we had come. Or of course you could just decide to stay. Poutu Heads itself is close to the entrance to Kaipara Harbour, an extensive area of water that stretches all the way up to Dargaville in the north and almost down to the city of Auckland itself. The Frenchman Marion du Fresne was the first European to identify the entrance to Kaipara Harbour in 1772 and he observed that at that time the land was uninhabited. We could have been in Auckland in just over an hour if there had been a ferry over to South Head, which by chance was our next random port of call. But Poutu seemed far more isolated than South Head since the last twenty or so kilometres of our journey was over gravel roads. The route from Dargaville initially passed through fertile horticultural and dairy land after which forestry took over as the terrain became more rugged. A small community, sufficient to support a small school, still exists in the Poutu area but what people do apart from forestry and farming I have no idea. It seemed an ideal location for some sort of artistic community due to its isolation but I failed to see any sign of it. A leisurely walk along the endless beach and even I managed to identify a number of the rare New Zealand dotterel. The sands were absolutely devoid of any other human presence and this brought to mind the Simon and Garfunkel classic, 'The Sound of Silence'.

But the peace of the place is currently under threat since there is a plan to install wind turbines at Poutu with a total capacity of 300 MW. I can certainly sympathise with the requirement for and advantages of clean energy but why here and why now? Surely if you have to have the ugly things install them in ugly places such as the windy suburbs of the cities that create the demand for energy in the first place. New Zealand politicians currently have a guilt complex about the country's ruminating cows and their theoretical contribution to global warming. However the cause of any future climate change is not here in New Zealand but in China, India and elsewhere but everyone is too politically correct to mention such delicate issues as the global population explosion, Chinese coal fired power stations being built by the score and the slavish pursuit of GDP growth rates. But as global demand for food expands exponentially the world will be imploring New Zealand to increase it's number of cows and as far as they will be concerned they can 'fart' as much as they like.

'Got it off your chest then Bro?'
'I think so'.
'Was there really a need for such language?'
'The spellchecker didn't seem to mind.'

The Maori legend of Poutu is that when Rongomai died his children decided to leave the settlement of Taporapora on the Mahuhu 'waka' (canoe). Those left behind felt resentment at their abandonment and by magic raised a storm that threatened the canoe. But the effects of the storm were most severe for the perpetrators since the waves cut off the peninsula and formed an island that then slipped into the sea taking everything and everybody with it. The disaster was known as 'Taraitanga', the shearing off. The name Poutu literally means 'to cut off'. In more recent times Poutu has been given the name 'The Place of Hidden Treasures' since the area encompasses vast stretches of unmodified dunes and wetlands, rare birds and plants, harbours, sand bars and shipwrecks. The information at the end of the road indicated that you could actually drive a four-wheel drive vehicle from Poutu

Heads all the way back up to Baylys Beach on the western sands. However the clear warnings of quicksand and other potential hazards for the unwary certainly put that option right out of my mind, even though Sas as usual was up for it. I had had my doubts about making the long trek down to Poutu, but no more.

Poutu Beach.

The Sands at Poutu.

The House on the Hill, Poutu.

16. South Head

There is an old picnic table on the beach at Mosquito Bay, South Head. The table has been fabricated from man-sized hunks of timber that a hurricane would not move. Rihapi, Unai, Di and Toa have been here and have left their carved imprint on the wood but their names will not be there forever since the termites have already commenced a feast that will last for a few more years yet. Nobody else was there apart from the peacocks and peahens which inhabit the small valley leading down to Mosquito Bay, their distinctive cries echoing about the place every now and again in the warm still air.

South Head sits opposite Poutu and together they form the entrance to Kaipara Harbour, which in terms of area is one of the largest harbours in the world. However all is not as positive as it seems since the entrance to the harbour is a treacherous stretch of water which is locally known as 'the graveyard' since it is full of shipwrecks. In Maori mythology the ocean going 'waka' (canoe) named Mahuhu sailed all the way from Hawaiki to New Zealand but overturned on the northern side of the entrance. The canoe was commanded by the tribal chief Rongomai, who drowned. His body was eaten by 'araara' (white trevally) and not surprisingly his descendants to this day will not eat that particular species of fish.

I had hoped to drive to the extremity of South Head but a farm gate barred our way. Plans are in hand to develop a South Head walkway but as far as I could see the plan must still have been in development since there were very few indications of signed paths to follow. A particular feature of South Head is the Woodhill Forest which stretches along the west coast a distance of sixty kilometres or more all the way from Muriwai in the south up to the peninsula of South Head itself. The main economic activities of the area have historically been animal and crop husbandry but more recently a number of 'lifestyle' blocks have been developed for citrus fruits, avocado and macadamia nuts.

From Mosquito Bay I looked across the water in the direction of Poutu hoping to see the exact place where I stood only yesterday but I could not locate it. Later I learnt that I was most probably looking at the Okahukura Peninsula instead, but we all make mistakes. Yesterdays golden sands at Poutu had been transformed here at South Head to black even though our other random location was so near. I noticed one or two sand flies but they were not in the numbers that would send people scrambling up the steep hill to the relative safety of their cars. It was an overcast day but still warm enough for shorts and sandals. A pair of trainers had been left at the entrance to a burrow of some kind, a kind of 'Jake was here' statement although probably Jake still has no idea where his footwear disappeared to whilst he was dozing. The sand reveals the footprints of many people but whether or not they were here yesterday, last week or one hundred years ago it is impossible to say. The water laps against the shoreline, the tide eddies and flows, tranquility reigns.

Mosquito Bay, South Head.

Burrowing Trainers, Mosquito Bay, South Head.

Picnic Table. Mosquito Bay, South Head.

17. Grahams Beach

There is no doubt that Grahams Beach was a surprise but in the most positive way. Looking at the map of the route to Grahams Beach it seemed to consist of a main north to south road with a series of minor roads leaving it at right angles to both the east and west at regular intervals. Due to its close proximity to Auckland I could only envisage row upon row of identical houses on their small plots of land, each struggling for the sun and air and that most unlikely of outcomes, a view of the sea. I pictured motels offering special rates but always showing the vacant sign, burger bars and video shops. But I was so wrong. From the moment I left Highway 1 the route was an absolute pleasure to drive with open countryside virtually all of the way.

In 1854 two pioneer families settled in the place then known as Te Kauri, one of the families was named Graham, and it was only after the death of the original Mr Graham that the place name was changed to Grahams Beach. From Grahams Beach itself you can look out over the extensive waters of Manukau Harbour and in the distance you can clearly see the Auckland Sky Tower, the central icon that oversees more than one million inhabitants. But here in Grahams Beach there is only silence, a row of pohutukawa trees line the golden sands, a few rather modest holiday homes await their owners and a large grassy reserve is open for all to enjoy. Even though it is a Saturday there are very few visitors here since it is a long drive from the centre of Auckland and there are many alternative beaches just to the north of the city where people used to crowds can find the company that they seek. Will Grahams Beach change? Should Grahams Beach change? Hopefully not.

On my return to Auckland I took a small diversion to the lighthouse at Manukau Heads. The views are dramatic and the dangers of the entrance are there for all to see, white flecked waves breaking over the shallow shifting sandbar. An information board tells the story of the wreck of HMS Orpheus in 1863:

'On the 7th February 1863 the Royal Navy vessel Orpheus was wrecked with the loss of 189 lives and this remains the worst maritime disaster in New Zealand's history. A steam corvette, HMS Orpheus, was based in Sydney to protect the South Pacific from possible attacks resulting from the American Civil War. On her fatal voyage she was to deliver supplies for naval ships in New Zealand and bring Commodore William Burnett to Auckland to meet with Governor General Sir George Grey, who had been requesting assistance to cope with impending war in Waikato. The ship's out of date chart did not show the correct location of the ever shifting sands of the Manukau Bar. Communications from the signal station - at that time on the northern side of the harbour - were slow, and misinterpreted by those on the ship. The Orpheus struck the bar in the early afternoon, and water started pouring in below decks. Of the 258 men on board - average age 22 - few could swim. They clung to the masts and rigging but as the hours went by most were swept away by the rising seas. Just before 9 pm, the last mast toppled, carrying with it 50 men and a stunned Burnett, who drowned. Rescue craft were able to save a few from the racing ebb tide but ultimately only 69 survived.'

Grahams Beach.

Pohutukawa Tree, Grahams Beach.

Sand Bank, Manukau Harbour.

Historic Lighthouse, Manakau Harbour.

18. Claris

When I drew Claris at random from the hat and found out where it actually was I experienced distinctly mixed emotions. Excitement about its location and concern about the costs of getting there, namely Great Barrier Island. But I had no choice in the matter since I was on a 'Mission from God' in Blues Brothers film parlance and you don't start this sort of thing and not follow through, do you? And looking on the bright side the random Claris selection could have just as easily been the Chatham Islands. Claris was originally known by the Maori as Kaitoke but the name was later changed to Claris in recognition of a Ministry of Works engineer who was employed in the construction of the airfield but later died in a plane crash.

I took some time exploring various possibilities of traveling to Claris which basically consisted of plane, ferry or a mixture of both. On Saturday the 4th December I drove to Auckland airport on the off chance that I could just jump on a plane and return by ferry or plane the same or the next day. The good news was that there was actually a seat on the plane in both directions. The bad news was that the flights were delayed. I initially thought that this was because of the winds but later I learnt that it was a sea mist which made take-off and landing on the island too dangerous. The thought of being stranded on Great Barrier Island for days was not a problem in itself, just the thought of the airport short-stay parking meter ticking over made me wince. Since flights could be delayed I concluded that a return ferry journey would be the best option but the company operating the service were not the easiest organisation to contact by phone or in person. Their offices could not be found at the main Viaduct Basin area and I was told that their offices were somewhere in Auckland, far from the waters edge. Therefore I concluded that fate had decided that Claris would just have to wait until the very end of my New Zealand odyssey and that I would visit Grahams Beach that day before heading south.

However, since I was staying that night in an Auckland backpacker I felt that I should give it one last try the following day, Sunday, even though I envisaged that return flight bookings would be tight on a weekend. But I just made it, since there was no problem on the outward 10.00 am flight and fortunately one seat remained for the 5.00 pm return flight. Fate had decided that I was going to Claris on schedule after all. The minuscule Britten-Norman Islander plane, with just five passengers and their baggage on board, clawed its way into the air, its twin engines making a beautiful, powerful, reliable sound. I was certainly up close and personal with the pilot since I was sitting directly behind him. Below the wake of numerous Sunday pleasure seeker boats made streaks of white on blue as they roared their way out from various marinas in the Auckland area. Waheike Island and the tip of the Coromandel Peninsula passed us by far below.

The initial impression of Great Barrier Island from the air was not that impressive since the native trees had clearly been fully exploited over the years and to tell the truth it all looked a bit scrubby. I had expected to see a number of exclusive homes and lodges for the rich and infamous but they did not make themselves readily apparent. Indeed it still seemed a place for lifestyle people, fishermen, artists, dropouts and those who had all the answers to the world's ills but whose only audience would be themselves. But it was the rugged cliffs, discreet sandy beaches and surf crashing into hidden coves that made the greatest impression from the air.

I had a general idea about the location of the Claris township and even I could tell that we were heading in the wrong direction. But all was well since it just so happened that we were making an intermediate stop at

Okiwi, just like a rural bus service. Soon, minus one local, we were back in the air for the short hop to the metropolis of Claris. Claris is quiet. In fact it is so quiet that you have to ask directions to find it. The pilots of the two planes had already strolled up the road for a fix of coffee before their return flights. Better than the two Lao pilots I flew with years ago who strolled into the terminal building for a beer during a short stopover. The walk along the road to Claris was through manuka and pine, apart from one or two buildings on the way that included an art gallery and a fish bait shop, and soon I reached the heart of the place. It all happens, or not, in a radius of about seventy metres in Claris, the Texas Cafe, Pigeon Post, laundrette, two petrol pumps, one of which was under repair, and a liquor store full to overflowing indicating that it helps to be an alcoholic to live on Great Barrier. Perhaps it is the isolation through dark winter months when the island may be cut off from the mainland for days. But then, that is also the attraction of the place.

I didn't expect to see much in the Claris settlement and therefore I was not disappointed. Great Barrier is a place for diving, fishing, surfing, trekking, horse riding, kayaking, swimming and mountain biking. It happens out there and not here in Claris. I still had a couple of hours to kill and so I took a walk towards what I hoped would be the distant Kaitoke beach that I had noticed during the landing. It was a hot and dusty walk but the effort was repaid one hundred times. Golden sand stretched far into the distance both left and right until meeting major rock outcrops against which the surf crashed and yielded. The place was a surfers paradise with curling waves, white topped over blue. Four or five swimmers appeared from the sand dunes, like a group of penguins off in search of a meal, but no other humans were visible. And so my impression of Claris had been dramatically changed from quiet backwater to ocean paradise in the space of an hour.

The plane was full for the return flight to Auckland airport and I was therefore promoted to the co-pilot's seat. I made a note of all the key controls in readiness for the heroic deed that I was sure that I would be required to fulfil.

'Auckland, this is Foxtrot Bravo. Co-pilot speaking.'
'Come in Foxtrot Bravo.'
'The pilot has collapsed and I have taken control of the plane.'
'How many flight hours do you have Sir?'
'Ten hours on MS Flight Simulator.'
'That will be fine. There seems to be a strange sound. Is that an engine malfunctioning?'
'Both engines are fine. It's just the other passengers panicking.'
'OK Foxtrot Bravo, I'm clearing Runway One for your approach.'

The landing was of course perfect and I waved to the fire engines as they raced parallel to the plane as we sped down the runway. The passengers were overjoyed, the press arrived but I casually walked away, collected Sas and drove on to my next random location.

Approaching Claris, Great Barrier Island

Kaitoke Beach, Claris, Great Barrier Island.

19. Tihiroa

As they say about the number nine bus, you wait ages for one to come along and then two arrive at the same time. The three previous random locations had been significant distances from each other but the next two selections on the list, Tihiroa and Honikiwi, were barely fifteen kilometres apart. No sign marked the location of Tihiroa as we arrived, just a windblown crossroads on State Highway 39, one road leading to Te Kawa and the other was encouragingly named the Tihiroa Road, no exit. The Tihiroa Hall, built in 1953, sits at the crossroads and seems to act as a testament to the place, a little shabby and seemingly underutilised, as if people have moved away or just lost interest. A livestock truck pulled onto the rough gravel area adjacent to the hall in a cloud of dust, unhitched the rear trailer, and departed rapidly somewhere else for its daily business, somewhere else but Tihiroa. Perhaps Sas and I would find the real Tihiroa up the no exit road but no, there was nothing of particular note to be seen before the turnaround point. It was clear that the location might require a bit of creative imagination. Perhaps, I thought, Tihiroa should be twinned with another place, Baden Baden might not be interested, but Otway might well be. In fact it may well jump at the opportunity. It is all too easy to be smug and condescending about the place. People live here, people die here, people make love here. Tihiroa is certainly not an unpleasant location to live, far from it. It is rolling sheep, beef and dairy country and the houses all look neat and tidy. I know five billion people who would jump at the chance to stake their claim there.

There is something impressive about the way that the country manages to protect the environment when involved in the potentially ugly matter of extracting coal from the ground. The Waikato coal region consists of thirteen coalfields with reserves of two billion tonnes and it just so happens that Tihiroa is one of those coal fields. The Pirongia coal seam, which lies below Tihiroa, is up to fourteen metres thick. However, to date, the field has never been mined but with an increasing global energy shortage the farmers and land owners in the region may be sitting on a fortune, just like Ma and Pa in the Beverly Hillbillies. And so sleepy Tihiroa may have the last laugh on Sas and Bro and still have it's pastures restored to their present state, if and when coal extraction is completed.

Community Hall, Tihiroa.

Tihiroa Road Post Boxes.

Tihiroa Landscape.

20. Honikiwi

There is something particularly attractive about roads to nowhere and the people that live there. The countryside around Honikiwi is little different from that at Tihiroa and yet it is so much more peaceful, distant as it is from the main highway and the lumbering trucks and mindless traffic. The road is under repair. It is a road to nowhere of any great significance and yet two large road rollers, a grader and water bowser are busy widening and maintaining the road. It seems to me as if road maintenance is a very positive method of providing employment and self-worth in the remoter areas of the country where employment opportunities are so limited. More a social service than an economic necessity perhaps but as far as Sas and I are concerned long may it continue. The men and women on the road do a great job, come summer sun or winter snow, and the money goes into areas and to people that really benefit, who really deserve. A little further on the Honikiwi Memorial Hall looked lonely with only a resting petrol tanker driver to keep it company.

A few weeks before we arrived in Honikiwi the peace of the place had been violently disturbed. The events which unfolded commenced with a local Honikiwi man being challenged by his neighbour as to why he was riding a motorbike that wasn't his. The suspect then punched his neighbour before pointing a shotgun at him and then speeding off. A short time later the gunman entered 'Curly's Bar' in Waitomo and demanded cash from the barman whilst threatening him with the same gun. A shot was fired but a number of customers leapt on the man and recovered the weapon, a very brave action, before the gunman broke free and disappeared. Police described the man, 187 cm tall, of medium athletic build and with a distinctive swastika tattoo on the left side of his face.

'So Curly, we know that he is a Maori, about 187 cm tall and of medium athletic build. Is there anything else that you can remember about the man?'

'Not really officer. Seemed like a pretty normal sort of joker to me,'

'Just think again Curly, any little clue will help us find him.'

'Well officer I know that it's pretty trivial but he did have a three inch Swastika tattoo carved into his left cheek.'

'Afraid that's not going to help us Curly. Since that Posh and Becks have been tattooing themselves all over the place three inch Swastika tattoos are two a penny.'

'Sorry officer, I was just trying to help.'

A few days later the man was arrested without incident. He already had an extensive criminal record but what was and is going on his mind who can tell.

A small graveyard sits on a hill close by to Honikiwi guarded by a solitary turkey. It is a sacred place to the Kites, Prestons and the others who lie there. A memorial catches my attention and reads:

'In loving memory of my darling. Did you ever know that you're our hero. You're everything in life our boys to be. If we can fly higher than an eagle you are the wind beneath our wings. Fly, fly high against the wind beneath our wings.'

And a poet once spoke in Honikiwi and still speaks to the hills, valleys and streams. What greater tribute can a beloved husband and father be given?

Honikiwi Welcome.

Post Box, Honikiwi.

Honikiwi Graveyard

21. Oeo

It was raining in Oeo, a light dampening of the ground more akin to drizzle, and it was the first rain that Sas and I had experienced in all of our twenty previous visits to the locations on our random list. You can usually rely on Taranaki for it to be wet and as a centre of dairying it needs to be. Oeo. Surely this is one of the few place names which is spoken as it is spelt, O.E.O? As usual there were no boundary markers to let you know that you had actually arrived in or left the settlement and it was therefore necessary to look out for rapidly passing signs to the Oeo stream, the Oeo 'pa' and the Oeo Road, which paradoxically pointed not to the settlement but away from the place towards Mount Egmont. Although Oeo is close to the sea there were no roads in that direction. It would have been enjoyable to have been able to have walked on the black sand and watch the surf crashing onto the beach.

The 1894 Hawera & Normanby Star newspaper makes it clear that sleepy Oeo was once a major centre of the horse racing world:

'Fine weather was experienced for the Oeo race meeting and the gathering was a decided success. It was estimated that there were five or six hundred persons present, a large proportion of whom were natives. The 'totalisator' was run by Mr F. Hill, and as the sum of £1020 was put through the machine, it is apparent that speculation was pretty brisk. The wants of the inner man were attended to by Messrs Knowles and Pellew of Opunake, who gave entire satisfaction. There were two or three good dividends, the largest being £31 10s on Nile in the

Consolation Handicap, but the money was not paid out. This was in consequence of a protest being made against the rider of the horse, who it is asserted was not qualified to ride because he had been ordered by the Metropolitan Club to 'stand down' for one month, and that time had not expired. The matter has been referred to that body for decision and in the meantime the money has been impounded.'

So controversy once reigned in tiny Oeo and no doubt many of those with the winning tickets made their views very clear to the race marshals especially as 'the wants of the inner man' had been well attended to. We could not determine the actual location of the old Oeo racecourse since there was nobody to ask, just two farmers speeding past on their individual trail and quad bikes, the farmers' friends.

In the second half of the nineteenth century Hone Pihama Te Rei Hanataua became the leader of Ngati Tama-Ahuroa hapu of Ngati Ruanui, centred on Oeo. Hone Pihama played a prominent part in land and business development at Oeo where he built a hotel and ran the Oeo to Hawera coach service. He was controversial among Maori because he stayed aloof from Titokowaru's uprising in 1868-69 and because he gave assistance in various forms to the government. The government considered him 'a returned rebel, and since his return a most active and trustworthy friend'. But through his political and business activities it was finally concluded that he left his own people better provided for materially than any others in Taranaki. In 1884 Hone Pihama built the meeting house Tipuahororangi at Oeo, which was opened by Titokowaru on 13 July 1884, perhaps illustrating that any past animosity between them had faded. Hone Pihama died on 1 April 1890 at Parihaka and the settlement of Pihama just north of Oeo is named after him in recognition of his service to the government and to his people.

We searched for something further of interest, something of character, and found a building sitting by the Oeo stream with all the hallmarks of an old tavern. But no longer, for today it is a private residence and the noise of late night drinking has long ago faded. Nearby to the former tavern sits the location of the Oeo 'pa' where history may or may not have happened. In July 1901 the iron barque 'Lizzie Bell' sailed from Wellington for Australia. She ran aground on a reef near the mouth of the Oeo stream. Although all eighteen crew were able to get into the lifeboat it was overturned by the heavy seas. Twelve seamen died of exposure before the rest could get help from local farmers. Ten bodies were recovered and were buried in the nearby Pihama cemetery.

A little further down the road a solitary flagpole stands and at its top flies a red flag with an insignia of some kind, too difficult to read or comprehend. It flies above a wooden sign which spells out 'Maolla' in large forceful letters. I like to think that this is a show of defiance from a Maori activist rousing the 'whanau' for one last battle but it is probably as mundane as the name of the farm. It sits by the side of the main highway adding mystery, evoking the last words of Citizen Kane, ...'Rosebud'.....'Rosebud'.

Oeo Landscape.

The Road to Oeo Pa.

Maolla, Oeo.

22. Upokongaro

It is a beautiful day in Upokongaro, the sky is blue, and a significant little settlement still remains after all these years. Just before reaching Upokongaro there are two historic place signposts, one to an old 'pa' and the second to the limited structural remains of an old brickworks. But for historic Upokongaro there is none and the motorist speeds on through, uninformed. St Mary's church stands proudly, just as it did in Burton's 1885 photograph. Alfred Burton described Upokongaro as follows:

'Though there are Maori Kaingas all around, Upokongaro is a white settlement and boasts a church with a three sided spire something like a bayonet, and a little theatre, where performs from time to time I understand, one of the cleverest little amateur dramatic companies in the Colony.'

A school remains in use but the old hotel no longer seems to exist, at least in its original form. The ferry crossing has long gone but I stumble upon an old wire rope and posts driven into the river bank which I sense is where the old river crossing was located because the banks on either side of the river are neither very high nor steep. Further up the river, adjacent to the church, a new landing has been built for the Waimere paddle steamer to drop off its passengers for a few minutes to enable them to snatch a few photographs before continuing on up the river. An information board stands on the landing and I assume that it contains a concise history of Upokongaro, but no, it is the bane of modern life, a long list of health and safety instructions about what you cannot do, not what you can do.

European settlement around Upokongaro, up the Makirikiri valley and towards Kaiwhaiki 'pa' proceeded throughout the 1850s and 1860s. A country hotel was first established at Upokongaro in 1866 where beer was served in tin pannikins out of a small lean-to structure. Within a short time a more substantial two storey structure was built and the hotel served the needs of the district for many years. The hotel was the centre of a bizarre incident in 1910 when a Mexican bushman, named Jimmy Laurent, became infatuated with one of the women guests. The woman told Laurent that she would 'run away' with him if he saved a certain amount of money. He gave her his pay regularly until it was the correct amount, and then she said no. So he placed gelignite around the hotel to blow it up but all the explosion did was break the windows. The bushman rushed down to the ferry boat which was tied to the wharf at one end and to a willow tree at the other. He let one end go and tried to row away but the fixed rope jerked him out of the boat and he drowned.

The ferry service had been established at Upokongaro in 1867 and it remained in operation until 1935. Throughout its history it was subject to considerable controversy because the wire which secured the ferry to either side of the river frequently obstructed river traffic and this led to clashes between the steam boat captains and the ferrymen. Matters came to a head in 1894 when two horses and their carts were crossing in the ferry when the river steamer Wairere travelled at speed towards the wire and only slowed down at the last moment. A tragic accident was only narrowly avoided. It seems that an illicit whisky still was operated for several years on a farm just above Upokongaro. The owner and operator of this plant, fearing a raid by the police, threw the still into a nearby swamp, where many years later their descendants unearthed portions of it which they presented to the Wanganui Museum. And so quiet Upokongaro has much history to offer the passing traveller, if only they knew.

St Mary's Church, Upokongaro.

Whanganui River, Upokongaro.

Severed Head, Upokongaro.

23. Jerusalem

Of all the random locations that I had drawn from the hat Jerusalem was the one that I had looked forward to visiting with the greatest anticipation. During my extended stay in New Zealand in 1974 it had already gained a reverential significance as the spiritual home and burial place of the poet James K. Baxter. The remoteness of the location, far along a gravel road up the Whanganui River, closer to Raetihi than Wanganui, made it even more attractive to those in search of somewhere special, somewhere where they could find themselves.

Why I had never travelled up that road in the past I can only put down to the fact that, like most people, I was on the way to somewhere else and a slow journey along the Whanganui River never really fitted in with my plans. Somehow I also had the feeling that the road was home to the laid back hippie community and that I would never feel comfortable with that spaced out peace and love ethos. For some reason I also felt that it must be one of the last refuges of the Maori disaffected and that the intrusion of a 'pakeha' would be resented as he made his voyeuristic journey through the area. It is strange how the mind creates its own image about a place and its people based on fragments of information, like pieces of broken pottery from an poorly executed archaeological dig.

The drive along the road running parallel to the Whanganui River is interesting without being spectacular. Occasional glimpses of the river gave an indication of what it could be like but they were few and far between. Perhaps the only way to approach Jerusalem is by the river itself but the drought and the subsequent low water level would have made that difficult at this particular time of the year. I hoped for an instant that jet boats had been banned from the river but then I found out that the Whanganui Scenic Experience Jet 'is an ideal way to experience and enjoy the beauty and serenity of the lower reaches of the Whanganui River, visiting key historic and spiritual sites'. Where now peace and tranquility? The canoe would be the only appropriate approach and in 1849 a colonial administrator, Donald McLean, and his companion Richard Taylor travelled up the Whanganui River to visit the tribes of the interior. McLean wrote how the *'sun pierced through the mist and reflected on the splashing of our paddles as each canoe in front was pressing up against the force of the fresh. Our own natives eagerly singing their shrill canoe songs and happily consoling themselves of arriving in good time in Hikurangi'*. Pure poetry that transports one back to the moment.

McLean also noted that 'At Pukehika a large clay-walled church had been built at Patearero'. Patearero, meaning 'slippery tongue' was the former name of a larger Maori settlement that incorporated Hirukarama, later more commonly known as Jerusalem. Long before James Baxter brought Jerusalem to worldwide attention it was the location of a catholic mission to the Maori. In 1883 Sister Suzanne Aubert arrived in Jerusalem to rejuvenate the faltering mission and to set up a refuge for destitute 'pakeha' children from Wellington. By doing so she gained the love and respect of the community. It was to this place that in September 1969 James Baxter and some of his followers came to create a more communal, loving and peaceful existence. However by September 1971 the followers behaviour had so upset the peace of the place that the local community, Maori, 'pakeha' and catholic mission alike, were united in their opposition. It was finally agreed that the James Baxter group was to be restricted to a maximum of ten persons. And so yet another idealistic dream had been turned sour by the flaws of human nature. James K. Baxter died on an Auckland street on the 22 October 1972, aged 46 years. Somehow I feel that he died a sad and disillusioned man, someone who had flown too close to the sun.

Jerusalem failed to speak to me when I finally arrived there after all these years. Perhaps I expected too much. Perhaps its time had passed by and it had reverted to the place that it should have been all the time, a quiet backwater of a backwater. But there was a benefit from the journey since further back down the river was Matahiwi where a Maori lady and her family were busy placing the 'River Queen' outside of their newly converted school house where local arts and crafts, and homemade cakes, were on display. There was a quiet beauty about the place. There were no cameras, no press, no hippie hangers-on, just them and their precarious precious venture. They were beginning to reclaim the river. I hope that they succeed.

Whanganui River, near Jerusalem.

The River Queen, Matahiwi.

Landscape, Jerusalem.

The Church at Jerusalem.

The Church Altar, Jerusalem.

24. Utiku

Utiku sits on both the main highway and railway line just south of Taihape. I knew nothing about the place on arrival but The Wool Company seemed to be at the heart of matters. A brief wander around the store failed to offer inspiration although the products on offer were clearly of good quality. It's just that the clear blue sky and the heat shimmer from the tarmac outside did not make one think of the need to keep warm, simply the opposite. A sign for Kells Wool Limited nearby informed all who wished to know that they were the local wool broker and so hopefully the pullovers, scarfs, socks and so on are all produced locally, but one can never tell. Whatever the case may be it was encouraging that such an enterprise existed in sleepy Utiku. I could not find the secret ingredient that I sought and so Sas and I took the road back in the Taihape direction and the first road right. Almost immediately we crossed over a narrow one-way bridge and I momentarily glanced down to see an amazing sight. A canyon, deep and narrow, cut into the earth as if by the axe of a Maori god of war. No sign on the nearby highway intersection revealed its existence, and yet, if there were, it would become a major tourist attraction. Add a simple viewing platform to the existing bridge, perhaps with a reinforced glass floor, and you would soon get people to put on their brakes and stop in Utiku. But perhaps the people of Utiku are happy just the way it is.

As I sat by the bridge recording my thoughts two young women came striding along. I had noticed them earlier on the main road and there was something about their demeanour which indicated that they were certainly determined but also tired. It seemed that they might welcome a lift to somewhere and when I asked they jumped at the offer. It turned out that they were both from Oregon on a month long visit to New Zealand and had decided that they would enjoy a long walk on such a beautiful day. They told me that they had already walked thirty kilometres and that their camper van was just over the hill. Taking the direction indicated we just kept going up and up and then we kept going down and down and in the end we travelled over eight kilometres, a really stiff walk for anyone. They had no idea that it was so far and since they had no water with them they were getting pretty dehydrated. But the real surprise was that their van was parked by an amazing canyon which turned out to be far wider and deeper than the one that I had seen before. And so the simple act of doing someone else a favour had led us, by chance, to another amazing hidden part of New Zealand. And so Utiku is not just a small settlement that should be passed by in a flash, it is actually a spectacular little area to spend some time.

An 1897 publication throws more light on Utiku and reveals that it 'first became a settlement in 1893, when a body of cooperative labourers, engaged on railway construction, was located there. Surrounded by native land, it was named after the original owner, Utiku Potaka. Further information about Utiku Potaka revealed that he was *'born at Otamakapua, Rangitikei, in 1836, and is of the Hauiti-Ngatiraukawa tribe. During his boyhood, which he spent at Waikato and Rotorua, he came but very little in contact with Europeans, and therefore he clings to the old Maori forms and ceremonies. When a young man, Mr. Utiku was several times fighting in the tribal wars, the last one of which was during the forties, at which time he met Sir Donald McLean. He also fought against the Hau Haus, and was with Colonel Whitmore's party. Mr. Utiku sees the great advantage of intercourse with Europeans, and is giving all his children a good education at the best schools. He has built a large ten-roomed house at Rata, and furnished his best rooms regardless of expense. The property at Rata, which is all cleared with the exception of a small clump reserved for firewood and timber, is fenced and subdivided.'*

The same source further revealed that *'At the recent census the population of the village was sixty-six, has a sawmill, two boarding houses, and a few homesteads. Mails are received and made up twice weekly, for both north and south, by the local postmaster. The township has already secured a public hall, and there is a comfortable accommodation house. The Temperance Hotel hostelry, which was completed and opened in May, 1896; contains seven bedrooms, two parlours, and a dining-room to seat twenty. The stables of five stalls and large loose-box are supplemented with an excellent paddock, which is specially available for traveling stock.'*

And so at the turn of the twentieth century Utiku was clearly an expanding community with an optimistic future ahead of itself. And with it's natural wonders there is no reason why Utiku should not feel the same way today.

The Wool Company, Utiku.

River Gorge, Utiku.

River Gorge, near Utiku.

25. Umutoi

The cock crows in Umutoi. It is once again a beautiful day and the drive up from Ashurst, running parallel to the Pohangina river, was a delight. This is a route that very few visitors would follow since the river cuts off any access to the west, whilst the Ruahine mountains restrict access to the east. The Pohangina river valley is therefore an idyllic situation known to just a few, with interesting tree shapes casting long morning shadows, a totara reserve for that majestic tree, isolated up-market houses sit above the flood plain with views to the mountains beyond, and a peaceful air is about the place.

But Umutoi itself is out and out sheep country, sitting high above the surrounding land, not particularly attractive in itself, seemingly tired and overworked, at least when compared to the river valley below. I read somewhere that Umutoi was named after a mountain but this is hill country. The settlement is small and a house, lovingly restored, sits awaiting a buyer. Perhaps the previous owner sought the solitude that Umutoi could offer but later found that they actually craved for company and companionship. You have to be born into this country, it is not a place for poets, artists or for those with the creative streak. It is a place for people who can endure harsh winters and live off the land, and what they produce is predominantly lambs and wool.

In 1909 a Feilding Star newspaper correspondent reported that:

'This is the mildest winter experienced in this district for many years, for which farmers are unfeignedly thankful. Grass is plentiful for this time of

year, and with every prospect of good prices for wool next season, settlers are happy....A well attended meeting was held in the schoolroom on Wednesday night to discuss the prospects of getting a creamery erected in Umutoi. Mr Hugh Osborne, chairman of directors of the Apiti Dairy Company, presided, and upwards of 200 cows were guaranteed in the room. After considerable argument over the vexed question of site, it was eventually decided to leave the matter entirely in the hands of the directors to decide at their meeting in Apiti on Friday evening. There is a large area of land suitable for dairying round Umutoi but with good prospects for wool, settlers do not care to abandon sheep altogether, preferring to have two strings to their bow, as it rarely occurs that wool and butter are both down together.'

And so the moral of the story is that everything in New Zealand changes but nothing changes. Farmers in Umutoi today are still the sometime beneficiaries and sometime victims of the vagaries of the global market. If they choose to change to dairying they can be sure that milk prices will plummet and if they continue with sheep farming they can be sure that their neighbouring dairy farmers will make a million. It was always a gamble and will remain a gamble.

Umutoi Farm House.

Shearing Shed, Umutoi.

Umutoi Landscape.

26. Crofton

The first place in Rangatikei District to be designated a town was Crofton where a general store cum post office was built and the land was divided into half acre sections. These were offered free to any person who built on them within two years. The only stipulation was that no liquor was to be sold from any of the premises erected in Crofton thus ensuring a tavern free township. Crofton was named after Sir William Fox's house of the same name but at one time it was known as Teetotal Township because of the restrictions on alcohol. Sir William Fox was premier of New Zealand on four separate occasions.

In 1875 a Mr A.C. Riggs, Boot and Shoemaker, advertised in a local paper *'to inform his friends and settlers in Crofton, Marton and surrounding districts, that he is just commencing business in the above line, and hopes by good workmanship and prompt attention to the commands of his patrons, to merit and receive a fair share of support'*. In 1886 a man named John Green became the storekeeper in Crofton but his journey to that point was interesting. He was born in Auckland but left home at the age of nine and was on the ship the 'White Swan' at the time when the seat of the New Zealand government was being transferred from Auckland to Wellington. On board the ship were several members of parliament en route to the embryo capital. The vessel was wrecked and young John Green's misfortunes led to his being taken into the service of Sir William Fox where he remained for twenty years, rising to the positions of butler, and afterwards of coachman. After a short time

John Green gave up being a storekeeper in Crofton and subsequently purchased land belonging to Sir William Fox closer to Marton.

When I randomly picked Crofton out of the hat I had no idea that I had actually passed through the settlement on many occasions in the past. The reason being that Crofton is located on a shortcut that I had taken many times on my regular journeys from Napier to Waverley, where I once owned a home. The Old Store at the Crofton crossroads is an impressive landmark but it now seems to have been converted into a domestic residence. It was difficult to park close to the main crossroads and so I chose a place about one hundred metres back down the road in the direction of Feilding. The house adjacent to my parking place had very high white fencing with a gate to match, a fact that only came to my attention just as I was about to leave. At that moment an old American type car drew up to the gates driven by a hulk of a man sitting beside a woman. The look that he gave me seemed to say 'Who the hell are you and why are you sitting outside of my property?' It was only then that I realised that I had parked outside of a particular type of residence and it certainly did not belong to the local tramping club. I left quickly and as I drove away I glanced briefly in the rear view mirror just in case I was being followed.

Crofton Landscape.

Former Lifestyle Bus, Crofton.

The Old Store, Crofton.

27. Gwavas

If anywhere exemplified the phrase 'hiding your light under a bushel' it was Gwavas. Highway 50 from Napier to Takapau has always offered a more preferable route south compared to the Highway 2 race track. It was a road that I knew well and the signpost marking the location of Gwavas had always made an impression on me, most probably because of it's association with the Welsh language, albeit that the origin of the name was Cornwall. Different places, same ancient language. Hidden by the trees a secret treasure was hidden from view for years at Gwavas.

In 1856 Major George Gwavas Carlyon, a veteran of the Crimean War, left his family home in Tregrehan, Cornwall, and with his wife Mary set sail for New Zealand. After initially settling in the Hutt Valley near Wellington the major brought his family to Hawkes Bay and bought Gwavas Station in 1859. George and Mary had five children, two daughters and three sons. Arthur Spry Gwavas Carlyon was the second eldest and it was he who laid out the gardens of the Gwavas homestead in 1880 and built the existing homestead in 1890.

At its peak Gwavas Station was a very successful business and comprised of 33,000 acres carrying 25,000 sheep and 800 cattle. Although remaining in the hands of descendants of the same family the main Gwavas homestead lay vacant for over forty years. Nothing was disturbed during this period and the original billiard table still had the original letter which ordered it. Breathtaking stained glass windows and an entrance hall and staircase of totara panelling were said to be particular features. In 2008 a family member took on the task of restoring the building back to it's historic category status and anyone seeing photographs of the internal and external features could not fail but to be impressed. Visitors and even guests were invited to see the restored homestead but then without warning in late 2010 the Gwavas homestead and 1000 hectare farm were put on the market before the iconic house had had a chance to introduce itself properly to visitors and passers-by. By February 2011 Gwavas Station had been sold for NZ 9.2 million to what were called 'Hawke's Bay farming entities', whatever that means, but if anyone spots Johnny Depp or Tom Cruise in the pub at Tikotino please be sure to let me know. For years I had passed that spot without being aware of what lay beyond the trees and now that I know there seems very little opportunity to see it. Oh well, onwards and upwards.

Landscape, Gwavas.

Entrance to Gwavas Homestead.

Gwavas Homestead.

28. Te Uri

Sas and I stopped briefly in Norsewood to see if the local cafe cum tourist office had any information about Te Uri. 'That's the place beyond Ormondville, isn't it?' was all that I could glean but the apple pie and coffee were excellent. Upon arrival in Ormondville itself the Te Uri Road sign appeared at a junction and we were clearly heading in the right direction. It may seem an unnecessary point to make but in New Zealand you can go for miles without seeing any signposts at road junctions. You just have to keep heading in what you believe to be the right direction. Just beyond Whetukura a war memorial remembered those from the settlement who had fought and died in the world wars. Many of the names had a distinct Scandinavian flavour in keeping with the ancestry of the early European settlers of the Dannevirke and Norsewood region.

And then we finally reached Te Uri, a fact confirmed by a signpost to the Te Uri Hall. The hall was of plain corrugated iron construction so typical of many rural settlements but it was of a later construction than most, 1958. Next to it stood a rural fire brigade building, no doubt manned by volunteers, and further up the road were stock pens. I was busy taking a few more photographs to record the visit when suddenly, in a cloud of dust, a livestock truck and trailer swept by and in one movement reversed up to the stock loading gate. At the same time a farmer appeared on his quad bike and without delay the driver and farmer started loading sheep onto the vehicle as though they were in a race against time. I approached to take more photographs and the farmer turned and simply asked *'Are you lost?'* I think that this just about summed up how remote Te Uri was and that it was not a place that strangers visited that often, unless it happened to be by mistake. The farmer, Bruce Williams, shot out his hand and I responded in a similar manner. The loading proceeded rapidly, ably supervised by Bruce's dog that was having a great time harrying the sheep along the race. *'He likes to bark at the sheep'* said Bruce as he gave his dog an encouraging pat. *'Cup of tea?'* and immediately Bruce was on the phone to his wife Angela, *'There's an Englishman here and I'm sending him up for a cup of tea.'* I think that I could have been a Martian and the same hospitality would have applied. *'Angela, there's a guy here from beyond the planet Zork. Better get the cake out as well since he's come a long way.'*

Te Uri is a typical remote Hawkes Bay settlement populated by hill farmers who live some distance from each other. It was therefore quite a surprise when Bruce brought out a comprehensive publication entitled 'Early Memoirs of Te Uri'. The book revealed that Te Uri was actually a very recent settlement since the first ballot for land in the area was not carried out until 1900 and it appeared that there were 1134 applications for just 40 sections of forest clad land. Among the successful ones were Bruce's ancestors. Of interest is the fact that women were only allowed to apply for half the area of land that men could request, a not unreasonable condition.

'How can you say that Bro, a not unreasonable condition. I'm female and you would only be a few kilometres out of Napier by now if it wasn't for me.'
'It was just a joke Sas. You know, a little light humour.'
'If that was a joke then I would stick to the day job if I was you.'

Sas and I said our goodbyes to Te Uri and headed off to our next random location.

Community Hall, Te Uri.

Stock Loading Ramp, Te Uri.

Livestock Transport Wagon, Te Uri.

Sheepdog supervising livestock shipment, Te Uri.

29. Coonoor

There is a much used saying that *'It is better to travel hopefully than to arrive'*. I think that this could be particularly appropriate for Coonoor because the journey to and from the settlement was full of unexpected surprises. The moment Sas and I left Te Uri the road turned to gravel and soon wide vistas towards the coast revealed themselves. Only then was it possible to appreciate how high we had climbed. The simple methodology employed on the random journey to date had been to identify a straightforward route from one place to the next without undertaking any research of the route itself or of particular places of interest on the way. But I noticed that a short diversion would take Sas and I to the beach at Porangahau where miles of golden sand and white rollers made it a surfers haven, then on past the longest place name in the world:

'Taumatawhakatangihangakoauauotamateaturipukakapikimaungahoronukupokaiwhenuakitanatahu'.

although the Welsh and others would no doubt dispute the claim. It appears that Tamatea was a well known chief, warrior and explorer of his time. He was the ancestor of the Ngati Kahungunu people of Porangahau, and acquired many names to commemorate his prowess. Whilst passing through the inland district of Porangahau, Tamatea encountered the Ngati Hine people and had to fight them to get past. In the battle known as 'Matanui' his brother was killed. Tamatea was so grieved at his loss that he stayed for some time at that place and each morning he would sit on the knoll to play a lament on his Koauau. Hence the name indicates *'the hill on which Tamatea, the chief of great physical stature and renown, played a lament on his flute to the memory of his brother.'* And then it was on to Coonoor via a short diversion to the Waihi Falls where a massive slab of rock drops water off the proverbial cliff. A relative trickle at this time of the year but in the winter or in a rainstorm, stand well clear.

The point to make about Coonoor is that it is definitely on the map since a signpost at a crossroads actually proclaims that it is one kilometre to Coonoor and sits on the Coonoor Road. The name seemed to conjure up visions of Indian hill stations where the expatriate ladies went to escape the heat of the plains during the summer, and where they could gossip, intrigue and romance. And so it is, since the place was actually named after an Indian town of that name. This Coonoor stands at the crossroads of a number of gravel routes but it appears that very few people actually live there. There were one or two houses in use but the remainder seemed to be in a state of decay, an indication of how few people it now takes to farm the land. I was told that there were glow worm caves at Coonoor located on private land but since I had already seen the Waitomo and Lake Te Anau caves in the past I felt that I had had enough for my lifetime, but I am possibly mistaken. No signs marked their location and there was nobody to ask. The land looked green and fertile and it was clear that the rainfall in Coonoor had been better than in Te Uri. I travelled a short way up a no exit road but there was little of significance to see. The rock outcrops bursting from the deep green grass were notable and the landscape was not at all unpleasant. It's just that the houses were in the valley bottoms and in winter, when the shadows were long, it must be a cold and dreary place to live. But it was time to move on to my next destination via the Piro Road.

The Piro Road soon turned to gravel and a sign quietly stated 'Unsuitable for Trailers'. Now the thing that you soon learn about New Zealanders is their capacity for understatement. For example, when describing the difficulty of a particular mountain climb they are likely to officially classify it as 'moderate' based on the fact that Reinhold Messner had failed on it twice. So when you see a sign 'Unsuitable for Trailers' you know that you are in for an interesting drive. At first we wondered what all the fuss was about but then we suddenly found ourselves on a very narrow road looking down a shear escarpment to the valley floor below. And the road went on for quite a few kilometres. I didn't plan this adventure, I was simply following what looked to be the most direct route to Alfreton and to Masterton beyond. The gravel road surface was actually good but time and time again we had to edge slowly around blind corners in case a local farmer, aware that few strangers would be mad enough to come this way, came haring around the corner. Apart from one farmer and his dog on a quad bike we encountered no-one but if two tourists met on that route it would be a long night trying to determine where and how they could pass each other. It was therefore with some relief, but with great satisfaction, that we finally made it to the main road leading towards my final destination of the day, Masterton. Usually I pride myself on my navigation skills but this time I turned left instead of right and headed off for fifteen kilometres in completely the wrong direction before correcting my mistake. In the remoter areas it is standard practice for drivers to acknowledge each others presence by the casual raising of the hand, after all they are probably neighbours. As I was speeding merrily along in the wrong direction I passed a farm on my right and in the adjacent field a youngster, a girl I think since the helmets make it difficult to tell, waved so energetically as she sped along on her quad bike going about her work with the sheep. Now there was a truly happy child.

Longest Place Name, on road to Coonoor.

Waihi Falls, on road to Coonoor.

Road Junction, Coonoor.

Landscape, Coonoor.

Abandoned House, Coonoor.

30. Bideford

I asked at the impressive tourist office in Masterton if they had any information about Bideford and the simple answer was no, with a suggestion that I might try the library. I felt that the answer that I had received was not at all negative since it simply reinforced the whole rationale behind our unusual journey since it demonstrated that even the locals often know little about their own district. We followed the road towards Bideford up the Tauweru river valley, an attractive area to be sure, and as we got closer to our objective a large wool shed appeared on our left and shearing was clearly in full flow. Loud rock music blasted across the sheep pens inspiring the shearers to finish just one more animal, and then another, and then another. The monotony and sweat drenched energy required would no doubt take its toll but the season is relatively short and the money is good.

As had happened before I began to feel that I had missed the settlement but then there it was. A signpost directed us to yet another community hall, this time the Bideford Hall. Another monument to those who fought in the wars sat directly in front of the hall but this one was particularly poignant. I looked at the individual names in turn and in the Great War only two men died, Norman Carswell and George Carswell. In the Second World War only one man died, but that man was named Norman Carswell. There were thirty names on the memorial and yet all of those who died were named Carswell. What grief must have been felt by the family, the mothers, sisters, brothers, cousins and friends, with the question echoing about the quiet valley, 'Why? Why us?' Yet their names are remembered in Bideford still and directly across the road from the monument a small primary school sits and perhaps this is where later generations of Carswells study?

We followed a gravel road out of Bideford to a junction where the individual signposts declared, Glen Crieff (no exit), Brookdale (no exit) and Awaroa (no exit). Rain threatened and then a few drops fell. It was time to turn around and we took another road from Bideford which soon turned to gravel with prospects of Glendonald and Alfreton beyond. Bideford was certainly a very pleasant place to live with it's feeling of remoteness and yet close to the large town of Masterton. As the rainfall intensity increased we left Bideford and a song came into my head, 'Brothers in Arms' by Dire Straits and I sang along in remembrance and gratitude of the Carswells. But somehow I felt that my visit had been lacking something and close to the sheep shearing shed I had seen a sign to Waterfalls Road and to the church of St Francis of Assisi. A closed gate barred the way and deterred, timid, I drove on past the shed but stopped again. I had to at least try to see if I could reach the church and so I turned again, unfastened the gate and drove over a small bridge and through some fir trees. Gates again barred the way, but there, on the right stood a beautiful little church, catholic I believe, because of the name. I stopped, walked around, viewed the small number of gravestones, but could not gain entry past the locked door. I peered through a gap and within there seemed to be an intimate exquisite scene. It was indeed Bideford Church. My visit was now fulfilled, I had found what I had sought.

Shearing Shed, Bideford.

War Memorial, Bideford.

Primary School, Bideford.

St Francis of Assisi Church, Bideford.

31. Ngatimoti

A short distance of sixteen kilometres from the bustling town of Motueka lies the settlement of Ngatimoti. Adjacent to the current Ngatimoti school boundary stands a small pyramid shaped monument with the words Nga Timote (1858-1958) which commemorates the centenary of the founding of the place. An early reference states that *'Ngatimoti originates from the carving of Na Timoti found on a tree about four chains below the meeting of the Pokororo River and the Motueka River on its eastern bank'*. This description of the location of the original tree is certainly very precise. A more recent but slightly contrasting version of the name origin indicates that a recently converted Maori Christian carved his name Nga Timote on the tree, but whatever the truth the name carving origin seems to be consistent.

John Park Salisbury was one of the very first European farmers to live in the Ngatimoti area. He had previously worked on farms in Australia but joined the rest of his family, who had arrived in New Zealand in 1853, in Wellington. He and his brother Edward subsequently moved to Motueka and shortly after they bought 400 acres at Ngatimoti. The purchase sounds straightforward except for the fact that at that time the area was virtually inaccessible by land. The brothers visited the area that they had bought by cutting their way through the bush and decided that access on foot was impractical. However by October 1854 they had built the canoe which they used to reach their property, a three day journey by water against the fast flowing stream. By the end of the following summer they had built a thatched mud hut and planted potatoes. When looking at this fertile area today it is difficult to fully appreciate the hardship which early settlers faced when developing a single acre of land to make it fit for agriculture. Every tree to be felled by hand, every tree stump to be forced from the soil, every drainage ditch to be dug, every rock and boulder to be removed, and all the time competing against flood, drought, pest and disease. And of course many failed, defeated by the thinness of the soil or their own physical frailties, driven back from land which they had for a short time been able to call their own.

Ngatimoti was our first location in the South Island and the sun shone on us. The construction of the Peninsular Bridge in 1913 created a lifeline for those on the western bank of the river but it is an area not commonly visited or even acknowledged by motorists speeding their way from Motoeka to Murchison and beyond. It was stated that the opening of the bridge was more important to those living on the far side of the river than the opening of the Panama Canal. And who can argue with that for roads and bridges are the vital arteries of early development in any country.

The Ngatimotu bowling club sits close to the river on the western side, neatly tended but devoid of players. In the distance tobacco kilns lie, quietly rusting against the backdrop of the Mount Arthur Range. We turned right at an intersection back towards Brooklyn, looking for something, and suddenly there it was. It was the most unusual post box that I had ever seen on my extensive travels in New Zealand, almost alien in design. At first I thought that it might be a tobacco or fruit juice press of some kind, being built as if it was to last for ever. A voice from above said, *'I bet you can't guess what that is?'* The man was of a similar age to myself and we began a game of questions and answers. *'Wool press?'. 'No'. 'Juicer?'. 'No'.* And so on until at last I had to gave in. *'It's a machine for putting brass eyelets in canvas'* he finally said relieving me from my agony. We talked a little longer about the floods that had hit the area in 1990 before I left. We did not exchange names, it wasn't necessary, but as strangers we passed a few easy minutes together.

Sas and I returned to the junction and instead of heading back to the bridge we proceeded straight onwards in the Pokororo direction where shortly the road and a giant fir tree, possibly a Redwood, actively competed for the same space. The tree had clearly won the battle since the road surface had buckled under the might of that wonderful natural force. We took the Big Pokororo Road, it disappointed, but further along its length perhaps it might surprise. We turned back and once more crossed the Peninsular Bridge to regain the eastern side of the river.

We then drove back along the main road in the Motueka direction to the Ngatimoti Memorial Hall where a plaque above the doorway honoured the fallen and a modern dazzling mosaic made a visual statement that may always remain a mystery to me. The nearby Ngatimoti store, founded 1941, sat devoid of people, stores and produce, testament to the precariousness of trade. Still we searched for that missing ingredient. The road that we followed was up the Orinoco Valley conjuring up images of Amazonian vistas and sultry heat. The road continued to climb and there we found the surprise that we had been looking for. It was not the picturesque St James's Church nor the war memorial, even though the first New Zealander to die in the First World War had come from Ngatimoti. It was Monterey House, a restaurant, tea house and golf course which sat in pristine condition totally invisible to the main highway. It could have been Kauri Cliffs, it could have been Augusta, it could have been St Andrews but it was Ngatimoti. So cross that river wherever that may be, take a left, take a right, journey up that gravel road into the unknown and embrace the surprises that your random journey has to offer.

Ngatimoti Bowling Club.

The Peninsular Bridge, Ngatimoti.

Alien Landing, Ngatimoti.

Monterey House Golf Club, Ngatimoti.

32. Six Mile

Six Mile is just what it indicates, namely six miles from somewhere and that somewhere is Murchison. Previously there may have been an actual settlement of a kind when gold miners prospected in the Six Mile area in search of their fortune in the late 1800s but any evidence of historic building structures had now long gone. In fact a school in Six Mile is recorded as being in existence in 1885 with a roll of fifteen and an attendance of ten but no evidence of early settlement remains. That is apart from the Six Mile hydroelectric power station and one or two new houses in the area. The small hydroelectric station was opened in 1922 and the occasion was marked by a public picnic, a performance by the Murchison town band, speeches and a banquet at the Commercial Hotel. And why not for the power station transformed life in the isolated Murchison area. The dairy farmers were able to replace their steam engines with much simpler to operate and maintain electric motors, the dairy factory used a considerable amount of electricity for milk processing, the streets of Murchison were lit with electric light and the housewives abandoned their kerosene lamps or temperamental gas lighting systems. The women were able to do their ironing without having to prepare fires to heat the old style flat irons and they could also do away with complicated charcoal or kerosene heated alternatives.

So much is made of alternative energy in this day and age that it is easy to forget that the practice of using natural forces is as old as the hills and that man has harnessed water and wind for hundreds if not thousands of years. The principle of hydroelectric power is simple inasmuch as water is either constrained by a dam or it is diverted at a gradual gradient until it can be dropped from a great height to power a turbine. The Six Mile station made use of the water races, pipes and water rights from the old Six Mile Creek gold claim. The power station operated for 54 years before it was deemed to be uneconomic and it finally closed down in 1975. The plant itself proved to be durable and generally trouble free. Floods, earthquakes, lightening and storms took their toll at times but the machinery was well looked after by successive engineers and worked well throughout its life. The generating plant has been lovingly restored and I have no doubt that it could be put back into action within a week or two if the water supply system could be resurrected.

The Six Mile Walkway to the head of the water reservoir is well marked and I was soon at the head of the main drop. The power and weight of water was such that massive concrete blocks were required to keep the large diameter steel pipe in place. I had noticed a Department of Conservation car where we had parked and the reason soon became clear. Two men were busy closing the track because there had been a substantial washout close to a footbridge and they were in the process of declaring it unsafe. The power of water had demonstrated itself yet again and I had no choice but to return to Sas. I had managed to take a few photographs of the station and the surrounding landscape and so basically I had fulfilled my visit to Six Mile but somehow there was something missing.

Might that something lie further up the Matakitaki river valley? The prospect looked enticing and although it was a gravel road we decided to go as far as we could before we had to turn around and retrace our steps. After a short distance a sign declared that the road was only suitable for four wheel drive vehicles and that six stream crossings were required on the route. What could be more inviting, as long as we were careful?

'What do you think Sas?'
'You know very well what I think. I'm disappointed that you even had to ask.'

We continued along the road under towering bluffs and past the Old Man of the Buller until we crossed the Matakitaki River at Horse Terrace. The river below the bridge raced through a dramatic gorge on its way to join the Buller River and then onwards to the sea. And still the road continued until we entered the Warbeck Scenic Reserve and started to climb through beech woods along a narrow but well formed road. It was only then that I turned the page of my map and found that, with luck, we might be able to make it right through to Burnbrae on Highway 65. Every so often I checked a ford on foot to make sure that the water was not too deep and also taking care that the road had places to turn should our path be blocked. Only twice did we have to remove fallen branches from the road to enable us to proceed. We had not seen any other vehicle tracks and so if we did misjudge a bend then it would be some time before Sas and I would be found. But that was the thrill of it all, what made pushing into the unknown so attractive. And then the saddle was reached and we knew that we were descending down into the Maruia River valley and towards the main highway. On arrival at Burnbrae the signpost informed us that it was fully sixty eight kilometres back to Murchison and yet another unexpected adventure had come to an end. We had seen areas of the country that few would take time to visit and we were definitely richer for the experience. As before on our journey random choices so often reveal beautiful secrets to those who take time to search.

Hydroelectric Power Station, Six Mile.

Matakitaki River, Horse Terrace.

The Road to Nowhere, beyond Six Mile.

33. Umere

The road from Karamea to Umere soon turned to gravel and in parts it reminded me of an English country lane. Umere used to be known as the 'Land of Promise' by the early European settlers and Arapito, on the other side of the Karamea River, was known as the 'Promised Land' indicating the hopes placed in them for the future. The sun broke through after the heavy morning rain and the temperature immediately began to rise. We stopped by the roadside to take a photograph of the landscape and a milk lorry and trailer drove past to collect their loads, for milking rarely ceases and this is dairy country. We actually drove through Umere without realising it until a fast flowing stream, entitled the Virgin Stream, blocked our progress. It sparkled in shade and light and tumbled away through the trees. I climbed out to assess the depth of the flow and the sandflies immediately welcomed me to their home. A road sign informed all who travelled to this point that the road beyond the stream was not maintained and that all drivers proceeded at their own risk. The Karamea Gorge track departed from this point but I was not sure how far it went or how hard it might be. We turned around since our objective was back in Umere and soon we spotted the path to the Big Rimu Tree. It was only a one hour return track and from what we had so far seen it must be the pride of Umere. The track to the Rimu was well graded and along the way the Department of Conservation had helpfully placed plaques at the foot of any tree or shrub of significance. Unfortunately I still had difficulty identifying the particular tree or shrub in question and I proceeded along the path no wiser. On arrival the Rimu was indeed a magnificent specimen and towered above the surrounding canopy. Great trees bring out a feeling for touch and I pressed my palm against the mass and wished it a long life. Hopefully I gave it some of my energy and I believe that it gave me some of its own. One can only hope that deep in the forest many other giant Rimu trees stand hidden from view, known only to a few. Umere never really did show itself to us since there was no school, community hall or any other sign of a distinct settlement. We returned to the backpacker whilst the Karamea River flowed swiftly by.

Once before I had travelled from Westport to Karamea and back in the day and I did not warm to the town then. I had thought that its isolation might offer a refuge for hippies and travellers looking for peace and enlightenment, similar to Golden Bay, but it does not. They say that West Coasters are 'characters' but as far as I am concerned the Karamean variety are simply miserable old sods. It seems that they are unhappy to be there and therefore make sure that you feel the same. A great night out for them is probably sitting at the bar not talking to one another. The backpacker that I had booked to stay in for two nights appeared to be in need of overseas aid and it was like entering the land of the living dead. My *'G'day'* was greeted with silent looks which seemed to say *'What the f... are you doing here.'* Well it was only for two nights and I had slept in some pretty rough conditions on my travels elsewhere in the world. The bunk room reminded me of Stalag Luft VI except that it was darker and danker, and I think that there was a dead body in the corner. Just one night rather than two I thought and brought in my gear. I had bought a roast chicken and all for Christmas dinner and started to put what I had in an overladen fridge. It all just fitted but at that moment two neanderthals told me that that was the woofers fridge and I was tempted to say *'Did you mean the tossers fridge?'* but they had their clubs with them and I wasn't quite sure if cannibalism had completely died out in the area. Somehow a night among the drongos didn't seem quite so appealing after that and so I cut my losses and departed down the road to another backpacker, a room of my own, and a good nights sleep.

Umere Landscape.

Rimu Tree Track, Umere.

34. Oparara

Oparara lies close to the sea on the coastal plain and the roar of waves breaking on the sandy shore seems to be permanent. It is clearly dairying country but somehow in the battle between nature and man it would seem that nature has won and it is not a particularly attractive landscape, except that is for the dairyman. There seems to be no central focus to the Oparara community since the farm houses are located far apart, but the cows seem content. A large greenhouse development sits isolated in the landscape growing tomatoes for a market which must be too far away but no other activity of note can be seen. The brown waters of the Oparara River flow swiftly to the sea where a battle begins between the fresh and the salt whilst the wind roars incessantly bending manuka trees to its will. And so the main Oparara interest must lie elsewhere and that place is the Oparara Basin.

The road into the Oparara Basin was well graded and like so many off-highway gravel roads the sixteen kilometres was a pleasure to drive. Along the way an empty beer bottle appeared on the road and a little further along another one. The tracks of a single car could be seen but it felt too early in the day for hoons to be up and about but it seemed as if they were. The walk into the largest natural structure, the Oparara Arch, was just so beautiful and ran adjacent to a tumbling river which alternated in colour from dark tan to coal black. Imagine a Disneyland Tropical Experience and multiply it by a thousand times and you may picture the scene. The Oparara Arch itself was on a gigantic scale bestriding the river which must have formed it thousands of years ago. It could only be described as cathedral like since that is just what it was. I retraced my steps and we drove the short distance to the Crazy Paving and Box Canyon Caves in an effort to avoid the hoons. The caves did not have a wow factor for me since I had already seen too many large holes in the ground for one lifetime. An empty bottle of beer lay at the foot of the stairs in one cave, another clue perhaps to an unpleasant encounter around the next corner.

The circular walk to Mirror Tarn and the Moria Gate arch took an hour and a quarter and it was such a memorable experience. As was my habit I spent minutes marveling at the reflections of trees and sky into the mirror like surface of a dark brown pool in the river, only to realise later that I had been worshipping at completely the wrong place. Nevertheless my photographs later proved that I was not so wrong to be impressed. When I finally reached it the Mirror Tarn was indeed an impressive sight but a slight ripple on the water's surface reduced its mirror like qualities. It was then onwards through the enchanted forest to the Moria Gate Arch. In my opinion it was actually more impressive than the far larger Oparara Arch because it was more in scale with it's surroundings. The path that I was on crossed over the top of the arch where moa footprints had been set in concrete paving stones. How lucky it was that a moa had actually passed by when the cement was still wet. A sign pointed the way to an alternative pathway to the arch that soon led into a narrow and slippery cave entrance that gave direct access to the whole area under the Moria Gate Arch. It was impossible to capture the amazing light which fell on the rocks, the gently flowing water and the trees. And then it was the short walk back to the car park. We had not seen a single other person from the moment that we had arrived in Oparara Basin until the moment we departed. Oparara had finally revealed her secrets to us.

'Holmes, as we were driving into the Oparara Basin I noticed an empty beer bottle in the middle of the road and a little further along another one.'
'And what else did you observe Watson?'

'I noticed the tracks of just a single vehicle and that on the bends the tracks tended to the left indicating that the car had recently travelled in the same direction as us.'

'Well done Watson. And what did you deduce from your perceptive observations.'

'Well I may be premature Holmes but I believe that there may be some unruly ruffians up ahead. Do you think that we should arm ourselves Holmes?'

'I trust that will not be necessary Watson. Look ahead, a green Nissan car is parked at the main car park. And what do you observe now Watson?'

'Clearly it is being driven by foreigners because it is a USave hire car and no self-respecting local ruffian would be without their own wheels.'

'An excellent observation Watson. Shall we drive on to the caves since that may yield some further clues.'

'By gad Holmes they are here already since there is yet another beer bottle. Protect yourself Holmes!'

'I think not Watson since the car that we have seen has yet to reach this point and there are no other cars here. And what does that tell us Watson?'

'Blowed if I know Holmes. It's a mystery to me.'

'It tells us Watson that the person or persons unknown in the Nissan are simple tourists like ourselves. Clearly the bottles that we have seen were discarded yesterday or on a previous day. I declare that they are therefore innocent of any misdemeanour Watson.'

'Great Scott Holmes, you're brilliant. I feel such a fool.'

'Indeed Watson, indeed.'

'Do you think that we should collect up the bottles and dispose of them in a suitable litter bin in Karamea Holmes?'

'The Department of Conservation instructions clearly state that visitors 'Should take only photographs and leave only footprints'. We are therefore obliged to leave the bottles where they are Watson'.

'Quite so Holmes. Quite so.'

River Colours, Oparara Basin.

Moira Gate Arch, Oparara Basin.

35. Roa

We took the secondary road from Greymouth to Roa and on the way passed places of historic importance in the coal mining world, Brunner and Blackball. The road from Blackball to Roa is only three kilometres in length but it had recently been widened and resurfaced to a standard suitable for a main highway but we could not understand why and soon, upon arrival in Roa, gates blocked any further progress. There were no signboards indicating what might lie beyond the gates, perhaps a coal mine or some other industrial development, but we had no way of knowing. High above in the towering hills we caught a glimpse of what appeared to be mine spoil. The three or four houses adjacent to the gates seemed to be in very poor condition but there were curtains in the windows and perhaps they were occupied after all. Whoever lived there was certainly not a well paid miner or skilled tradesman and Roa had the feel of a settlement on the edge of extinction. Perhaps the Appalachian coal mining district in the States has the same feel? Turning back towards Blackball a small farm structure sat close to the road, a barn of some kind of Swiss or Austrian design, perhaps the handiwork of an early settler from those parts. Roa is at the end of the end, hemmed in as it is by tree clad slopes steeply rising into the clouds. The sound of fast flowing rivers and streams filled the air on both sides of the road but trees masked them from sight. The heavy morning rain had passed but the sky remained dark and sombre.

Further back towards Blackball a signpost revealed the existence of the Croesus Track and Sas headed in that direction sensing some new adventure along the way. The road rose steeply at first and in a gap in the trees I briefly glimpsed Roa far below. The Croesus Track itself passes through the beautifully named Roaring Meg ecological area all the way to Barrytown on the Punakaiki coast. A recent rockfall partially obstructed the road and I became nervous less Sas and I got trapped by a new fall but Sas just ploughed on determined to make the full five kilometres to where the walking track commenced, no matter what. And then at last we were there, a solitary tramper's car sat forlornly in the rain, the well formed path led off to the heights and we returned, somewhat disappointed, towards the main road. For a few seconds we stopped again to look down on Roa and I noticed that there were in fact a number of houses hidden from view from the newly paved road. Hidden, as it were, from the prying eyes of strangers and government officials.

The mystery of Roa gripped me and on my return to Greymouth I at last discovered what lay beyond those gates. Commencing with a preliminary geological survey in 1904 the Paparoa Coal Company had begun mining, in what is today the Roa mining area, in 1907 and continued until 1971 when mining ceased. By then over 1.6 million tons of coal had been extracted from the two major coal seams, the Morgan and the Kimbell. Francis Mining Company Limited acquired ownership of the mining licenses in 1988 and extended the open cast workings, extracting a further 250,000 tonnes until the surface workings exhausted the reserves in 1995. Since 2001 the Roa Mining Company had been carrying out important expansion programs. This had included the opening of new access drives to the coal reserves and the construction of a primary wash plant and a workshop. Underground and surface development work therefore continues to this day at Roa. And so there we have it.

Sadly on the 8th September 2006 a miner was killed at the Roa mine, as reported in the NZ Herald News. *'A miner died today after he was trapped when a tunnel collapsed in the Roa coal mine near Blackball on the West Coast. Acting Senior Sergeant Craig Shannahan of Greymouth police said the 47-year-old man's body had been recovered late this afternoon. His family has been advised, the coroner will be informed and the deceased's details will be revealed no later than tomorrow. The miner was trapped after a shaft in the mine, about 800m from the entrance, collapsed just after 11a.m. Nine other miners working at the site escaped unscathed.'* The man who died was forty seven year old Bernard Green, nicknamed 'Hercules' by his workmates, who had represented New Zealand at rugby league and scored two tries on the Kiwis 1980 tour of Great Britain and France. In later years he became a champion coal shoveler, and he and his large family were well-known in Runanga where they lived, and in nearby Blackball. Trevor O'Neill, a teammate of Mr Green in the Runanga rugby league club the Seagulls, said Mr Green was a great man of phenomenal strength. *'He could just pick stuff up on to his shoulder and away he'd go. His loves in life were his work and league. He coached a local team and his wife was also involved in the club. Mr Green had been a miner all his working life and appeared unfazed by the risks.'*

A recent photograph of the Roa mine staff shows just fifteen men whilst at the time of Bernard Green's death twenty men were employed. When I think of coal mines I envision large enterprises employing well over one hundred men but this mine is small and intimate. And therefore the loss of Bernard Green, as with the Pike River miners, will have been felt deeply within the small community where they lived, worked and played.

Old Farm Structure, Roa.

The Road to Roa.

Brunner Mine Disaster Memorial, Brunner.

36. Ngahere

Our visit to Ngahere was not looking promising since it had rained continuously throughout the previous night and the Grey River was in full flood. Full flood does not adequately describe the torrent that was flowing beneath the bridge which marked the location of the 1896 Brunner mine disaster where 65 miners had perished. Enormous tree trunks in the river were being flung this way and that by the tumult and anyone unlucky enough to be caught out by the flow that day would not have survived. Just before Ngahere traffic was turning back from a flooded section under a railway bridge but Sas just ploughed straight on through much to my discomfit. And on the Ngahere boundary the local volunteer fire brigade was on hand as the water flowed across the main road and through a house but there was little they could do other than direct the traffic. The house occupants seemed very philosophical about the situation and it was only later that I discovered that the house was the home of one of the men who had died in the recent Pike River mine disaster. Clearly a little water had no significance to a family that had already suffered too much.

I found out this information in the Ngahere tavern where I had, without success, gone to seek a coffee and settled for a beer. The pub was empty at that time of day and the landlord was somewhat reticent to discuss what Ngahere had to offer to a stranger. Perhaps he was tired of reporters from all corners of the world seeking their own award winning angle on the Pike River tragedy to file back to Tokyo or New York. And what else would a stranger be seeking in Ngahere on such an awful day? But only the day before Ngahere had made the news in the Greymouth Star. It seemed that some local youths had been running amok in little Ngahere and were making the life of many residents a misery. The general mayhem had continued over a six month period and culminated in the burning down of a bach on nearby Redjacks Road. The police had visited the township on a number of occasions but the locals had had enough and were going to sort the problem out in their own West Coast way and I'm sure that they will. Pity the hoons.

Just when I thought that Ngahere had little of interest to offer I discovered that on the far side of the Grey River sat the 'Kanieri', a 3,500 tonne gold dredger, the last one in New Zealand and one of few remaining gold dredgers in the world. The 'Kanieri' had had a long and distinguished career since the original dredger had been built in 1938 for the Kaniere Gold Dredging Company. By 1953 the dredger had recovered 175,000 oz of gold from the Hokitika area after which it had been moved to the Taramakau River north of Hokitika where it had extracted a further 202,000 oz by the time that it ceased operation in 1978. The 'Kanieri' was then laid up and a major refit was undertaken at a cost of NZ $30 million. Unfortunately after the refit the dredger did not work well and combined with unsatisfactory gold prices it meant that the Australian owners went out of business.

In 1990 the 'Kanieri' was bought by a man named Allan Birchfield and after another refit it worked successfully for a further twelve years at Ngahere before once again being laid up in 2004. As gold prices rose above the US$ 1,000 per oz level the viability of dredging for gold was once more positive and the 'Kanieri' was again put to work in 2009. The dredger currently provides employment for a staff of fifteen working two eight hour shifts and seven days a week. It is estimated that the 'Kanieri' probably extracts between 5.000 oz and 7,000 oz per year which at a price of US$ 1,300 per oz equates to a potential gross income of US$ 6.5 million to US$ 9.1 million per annum. However gold dredging is put into perspective by the fact that 1,000 tons of gravel has to be processed to obtain a single ounce of gold. For how long the 'Kanieri' can keep operating depends on the price of gold and the high costs of maintaining the dredger. In the meantime little Ngahere is certainly on the map as a gold mining location of national and even international importance. And so once again a sleepy little random location has thrown up yet another unexpected surprise.

One Careful Owner, Ngahere.

Flooding at 'Try Again Road', Ngahere.

37. Jacksons

The approach from the coast to Jacksons along Highway 73 was like approaching the mythical Gates of Doom with the Hohonu Range closing in on the left and the Bald Range on the right, their summits lost in clouds. Without warning we turned a corner to be greeted by the road sign for Jacksons and a little further along the historic Jacksons Tavern, established 1868, appeared in view. When I asked the lady in the Greymouth tourist information centre the only thing she could tell me about Jacksons was that it had a pub but little else. But what a gem the pub turned out to be with a large open fireplace and logs blazing. The floor, ceiling, tables, chairs and bar were all of wood giving the place a warm homely feel. I ordered a small beer and the pub speciality, 'Peas, Pie and Pud', which consisted of a pork and kumara pie sitting on mashed potato and a bed of garden peas, then topped off with gravy. It looked a work of art to a hungry traveller. The atmosphere of the place was overwhelmingly friendly, a local pub but with an open invitation to all passers-by. It was Boxing Day lunchtime and as each local character entered they greeted each other warmly. The tavern and settlement both take their name from Adam and Michael Jackson who built their first pub on or close to the present site in 1868. The original pub was washed away in what was called the Old Man storm but continued to operate under a tarpaulin shelter until a replacement was subsequently completed in 1872. The existing tavern was built in 1910 and although modernised in recent years it still retains a traditional charm. When Jacksons Tavern first opened it drew much of its custom from gold seeking prospectors from Canterbury who were making the treacherous five day journey on foot via Arthurs Pass to the gold fields in the west.

On one wall of the pub I discovered two framed photographs of soldiers in uniform, in memory of Charles Debenham and Henry Edward Debenham, both citizens of Jacksons. Charles died at Passchendaele in Belgium on Sunday 17th June 1917, aged 23 years, and Henry died at Messines in France on Friday 12 October 1917, aged 28 years. It is approaching one hundred years since their deaths and yet rightly they still have their place of honour in Jacksons. I assumed that they were brothers but I did not ask.

In the valley below a rail and road bridge both cross the Taramakau River with its glacier melt milky white blue waters making their turbulent way to the sea. Everything was on a massive scale here but the valley floor was wide and fertile allowing significant agricultural production. On our return journey to Greymouth we crossed the road bridge and took the route back to the coast via Mitchells and Lake Brunner. For the most part it was uninteresting but the gravel roads are always fun to drive.

I think that it is natural but when I looked in advance at some of the locations that I was to visit I sometimes felt a sense of concern that the place in question would be drop dead boring with not a single feature of interest. I felt that about Jacksons but I should have known better by now and Jacksons, set among majestic mountains as it is, had much to offer. And by the way the 'Peas, Pie and Pud' was excellent. Don't miss it if you happen to pass this way.

'Hey Dad! Historic tavern, five hundred metres.'
'Wad'ya say son?'
'Historic tavern.'
'Sorry son, we've passed it now. Last time your mum and I drove from Christchurch to Greymouth we did it in three twenty. I'll beat that time this year if it kills me.'
'Or us Dad.'
'Sorry son, wad'ya say?'
'Nothing Dad. Nothing.'

Jacksons Tavern.

Landscape, Jacksons.

38. Herepo

We left Greymouth heading south along the Glacier Highway in search of Herepo. My limited research had revealed no information about the place whatsoever. 'Say No To Drugs' is a widespread plea nowadays but I thought to myself 'Who Needs Drugs?' as I cruised through the Pukekura Scenic Reserve with Pink Floyd blasting out of the CD player. On the map the block-like structure of the road layout around Herepo indicated dairy country close to the Wanganui River. And indeed it was, a significant area of flat land in a mountain region where flat land is at a premium. Initially many fields seemed to consist more of weeds than grass but as I drove closer to Herepo itself the pasture improved. Jersey or Guernsey cows munched contentedly on the grass sward and the sun shone warmly on their backs. A farmer and his son were trying to recover three milking cows that had escaped onto the road. The sheep dogs yapped energetically but the cows seemed to be winning and the last that I saw of them they were all heading in the wrong direction.

An attractive young women on a horse ambled towards us and I asked her about Herepo. She told me that there used to be a dairy factory there in the past and that Herepo was in the process of being recognised as a township or some type of formal settlement. *'Oh and by the way'* she said as an afterthought *'Herepo was where Menzies landed his plane.'* Her words vaguely reminded me of a historic flight from Australia but when and who was actually involved I did not know. I certainly didn't know that the flight had any connection at all with Herepo. And so yet again it had happened. I had been looking for a metaphorical hook to land something of interest in yet another of my random locations and this time I had landed a real monster game fish.

The beauty on the horse continued on her leisurely path and I returned to Hari Hari where she had told me that an exhibition of the flight could be found. A replica of the plane sat within a specially constructed shelter and the open cockpit plane was minute. The first item that I read was a letter written by Guy Lambton Menzies before he made the flight and I felt that it captured the spirit of his character.

'Dear Norm,
I am sorry to have kept my real destination from you and I know that, if you had known where I really intended making for, you would have tried to prevent my going. I am flying to New Zealand instead of Perth as I planned with you. I have always wanted to do this trip and the opportunity presented itself, I did not hesitate about taking it as I feel perfectly confident about getting there. At any rate you might wish me luck, Cheerio, Guy.'

Guy Menzies was determined to make his mark in aviation history and he therefore decided to make the first solo flight across the Tasman Sea from Australia to New Zealand. No life raft was on the flight carried out in an Avro Avian biplane named "Southern Cross Junior" and he did not have official permission for the attempt. Just before 1.00 am on the 7th January 1931 Menzies took off from Mascot Airport near Sydney. After encountering very severe flying conditions he finally made landfall close to Gillespie's Beach, a place that had been a gold mining settlement in the 1860s. Flying above the seaside settlement of Okarito and seeing people below Menzies scribbled a note, crammed it into a bottle and threw it out with a message asking *'Where can I land, point to nearest town on the coast'* but the bottle broke and the message was lost for many years. Turning inland at the Wanganui River mouth, and with dwindling fuel supplies, he mistook a flax-covered swamp for farmland, circled and came into land, but unfortunately the aircraft turned head over heels.

Uninjured Menzies then tried to make his way to one of the farm houses that he had seen from the air but soon met Jack Hewer who demanded

'Who the bloody hell are you?', a typically straightforward Kiwi greeting if ever there was one. Menzies then travelled from Hari Hari to Ross with Bert Kelly in his cream truck, even stopping to collect cream urns on the way. News of this amazing solo flight soon spread throughout New Zealand and Australia and the historic event was reported in a Sydney paper the very same day. Guy Menzies was just twenty one years old.

We then drove to the actual site of the landing which was a short distance from Herepo, close to the Wanganui River and adjacent to a fast running clear mountain stream. A trout fisherman was busily preparing his equipment for the day's sport. I felt that I had gathered enough information about Herepo but Sas insisted that we explored to the mouth of the Wanganui river. It was a rough gravel road and as we got closer to the objective a number of bachs could be seen tucked away and many had cars parked beside them. Perhaps it was a remarkable whitebait or trout fishing river, but I had no way of knowing. We finally arrived at the roads end and Sas waited while I walked towards the sea but it turned out to be too far for the time that I had available and I retraced my steps. The Wanganui River ran swiftly by laden with snow melt, the sky above was pure blue, but the spectacular mountain views, which surely there must be, remained hidden by clouds.

Herepo Landscape.

Menzies Landing in 1931, Herepo.

39. Luggate

A short distance from Luggate the mighty Clutha River runs forcefully below the Red River Bridge on its long journey to the sea. In early 2010 the bridge was in the process of being repainted and the scaffolding on which the painters were working had been covered in fabric to provide the workers with protection against the bitterly cold wind and rain. One of New Zealand's major energy providers, Contact Energy, had a year previously outlined various options to dam the river at four locations, Tuapeka Mouth, Beaumont, Queensberry and Luggate at an estimated cost of NZ$ 1.5 billion. An alliance of several groups opposed to further dam construction on the Clutha River, the Clutha River Forum, immediately launched an Option 5, namely no more dams on the river. On the 31st March 2010 the painting contractors arrived at the site to discover that their fabric had made a very convenient canvas for a huge protest banner proclaiming 'NO MORE DAMS' for the full width of the bridge. A motorist later reported having seen a group of people on the bridge after midnight but thought that they were contractors working overtime to finish the work before Easter. Nobody claimed responsibility for the protest but whoever was responsible was certainly very brave to undertake the work in the dark and over a raging torrent. A spokesperson for Contact Energy immediately stated that the company was appalled by such *'blatant environmental vandalism'* and no doubt that spokesperson was soon looking for another job for failing to see the irony of their statement.

And so two of our randomly chosen locations, Luggate and Queensberry, were at the centre of a debate which is being repeated all over the world, namely the conflicting requirements of energy demand

and environmental protection. Sas and I drove down to the river to take a closer look and the bridge was certainly an impressive structure. The impact was amplified by the beautiful deep red colour contrasting with the ice blue water running beneath it.

'So what do you think Sas, dam the Clutha or not?'
'Dam the river I say. All that free clean energy. How can anyone object?'
'But look at it Sas. It's an absolutely amazing stretch of water. It's what the people who appreciate the beauty of nature come to see and once its gone its gone.'
'There are plenty of other spectacular rivers in New Zealand. Without sufficient energy the country's pretty stuffed for the future as far as I can see. And the alternative sources such as coal and oil are much worse. Start building now I say.'
'But why does the country need more energy in the first place? The population is still small and with modern technology and the internet there is no reason why New Zealand needs any more people. However, I do see your point. What with escalating fuel prices I guess that more electricity generation would mean that we could have more electric cars to reduce pollution and at least that would allow you to gracefully retire to the knackers yard in the sky.'
'Now hold on a minute. I gave reasons why I might be for the dams but I hadn't completely made up my mind. On second thoughts, and taking everything into consideration, I guess that you're right Bro. Let's just leave things the way that they are.'
'I thought that you might see it my way.'
'You set me up, didn't you?'
'Possibly Sas. Possibly.'

Luggate has the misfortune, or possibly good fortune, to be located on the main highway only twelve kilometres from Wanaka. It is therefore too close to Wanaka for any speeding motorist to consider stopping for a break and by not doing so they miss out on Luggate and the delightful Luggate Hotel. The hotel has a similar feel to the popular Cardrona Hotel since they have real character, both inside and out. St David's

Presbyterian church sits close by prettily decked out with the characteristic red roof and white walls whilst the Upper Clutha Transport Company provides an injection of industry for the community and no doubt income for the pub. As everywhere sections are for sale in Luggate but if I were a local I would like it to stay just the way that it is.

The Red River Bridge, Luggate.

Cottage, Luggate.

40. Queensberry

'Man you look rough Bro.'
'Not so loud Sas. I didn't get much sleep last night.'
'Celebrating in the New Year too hard, ay. Good on yer Bro.'
'No way. I was in bed by eleven. You know I told you that I would be sharing the backpacker room with five members of the Maori band performing at the Albert Town pub.'
'Cause a bit of a rumpus did they? Those boys certainly know how to party.'
'No, not a bit of it. They cancelled at the last minute since they had found somewhere else. I ended up having to share with three young Czech girls.'
'Man, I didn't think you still had it in you.'
'Hold on Sas. You know it's not like that in the backpackers. It was the Kiwi guy who came in from the pub at two in the morning. Nice guy but man did he snore. At about four o'clock the three Czech girls decamped with their sleeping bags to the lounge. The next morning they told me that they had never heard a real snorer before.'
'What about yourself Bro?'
'After all these years in backpackers you just get used to it. I just thought that it was tiring but amusing.'
'Ah, budget backpacker life. Don't you just love it.'

Queensberry is for sale. 'Your dream awaits you at Queensberry Hills, Wanaka', a billboard next to the main highway proclaimed when in fact Wanaka was a full twenty six kilometres away. Yet more PR promises of 'freedom' and 'happiness' if only John, if only we could raise the extra funds to buy a section at Queensberry Hills. There will be no shops or services there but the happy purchasers can sit and admire the view for hour after hour after hour. And as the years pass the sections around them will be sub-divided, their views obstructed and yet another round of disappointment will fall on those whose dream had long ago faded. And, of course, it was always just a dream.

The sheep grazed in vast numbers on the Queensberry terrace high above the swift flowing Clutha River whilst small sprinkler irrigators battled to keep the grass green in this dry rain shadow land, with minimal success. The LazyDog Restaurant and Wine Cellar offered passers-by yet another unique wine tasting experience but trade must be difficult away from the towns. Perhaps the establishment of the venture was yet again just the fulfilment of another dream. And the irony was that the LazyDog seemed to dislike dogs intensely as a sign forbade dogs beyond the entrance to the compound.

Returning in the direction of Wanaka the Queensberry Inn offered yet more 'unique experiences' in terms of historic stone cottage accommodation but it all looked rather quiet and perhaps the venture had already followed the path to closure of it's ancient predecessors. Although Queensberry had never been significant in terms of gold mining activities it was an important staging post for travellers to and from the gold fields. There used to be a twice-weekly coach between Dunedin and Pembroke, the previous name for Wanaka, and it was the place to stop for coaches and supply wagons. The premises, variously known as Kidd's Hotel or Woodhouse's Hotel depending on the licensee, handled up to eight wagons and a hundred horses at any one time. The hotel replacement, the Queensberry Inn, flourished into the 1920s until the demand for it's services finally ceased. If there is one thing to be learned from this random journey it is that nothing is permanent, that circumstances change and that if you don't rapidly adapt you will be left far behind.

'A bit hard on the folks of Queensberry weren't you Bro?'
'I guess so Sas but when will all this building development stop? It's only the property developers that will gain, not the people nor the country.'
'Well at least the sections are not selling at the moment.'

'They will Sas, over time they will.'

Queensberry Landscape.

Everything for Sale, Queensberry.

41. Lumsden

Lumsden is ideally situated at the crossroads of routes to Queenstown, Dunedin, Invercargill and Te Anau. Originally the district was known as The Elbow and when that name was given to the newly constructed railway station the residents of the settlement of Castlerock on the other side of the Oreti River, then also know as The Elbow, objected and the matter was brought to the attention of George Lumsden of the Otago Provincial Council. In the absence of any other suggestions the Railways Department named the station as Lumsden and the settlement subsequently took on the same name. In the past Lumsden used to be a major railway junction but by 1982 all railway connections to the settlement had been closed. In 1905 Lumsden had a population of 300 and at that time could boast three hotels, two blacksmith's shops, two general stores, two bakeries, a butcher, a bootmaker and a tailor. The principle products produced in the area were wool, cereals, rabbits and dairy products.

The current Lumsden Hotel had an impressive 'Southern Man' mural which was beautifully executed and should have enticed any traveller to stop for a break on their journey. However the facade of the hotel was now slowly crumbling as if the original driving force behind the project had long departed. In the early 1900's the Lumsden Hotel was named the Railway Hotel and offered twenty-seven rooms, including nineteen bedrooms, four sitting rooms, two dining-rooms and a billiard room. The hotel stables had twenty stalls and the proprietor, Joseph Crosbie, ran two coaches per week from Lumsden to Lake Manapouri via Te Anau. The extent of the hotel and its activities provides an indication of the hopes for the future that must have existed in Lumsden at that time.

Unfortunately Lumsden now felt like a theme park that had lost it's theme. The railway station is such an attractive structure and would have made a wonderful cafe or restaurant but at the time of our visit the building was closed, even though it was the designated Lumsden information centre. The only motel in town was for sale and the nearby campsite was devoid of any custom. An internet guide summed up Lumsden very well when it stated *'Lumsden attracts only a small number of travellers and those visiting the area might want to check out some more popular nearby destinations such as Queenstown and Te Anau. The takeaway place does some pretty good chips'*.

Lumsden Hotel.

Railway Signalling, Lumsden.

42. Josephville

The name Josephville seems to imply that there once was a settlement worthy of being called a 'ville' at the location but upon arrival no sign of a memorial hall, primary school or any other clue to community existed. The Oreti River sparkled as it flowed past close by, laden no doubt with sporting trout of epic proportions. The view from a hill to the south of Josephville yielded panoramic vistas over a vast fertile plain and it was certainly a beautiful sight on a hot summers day. On distant hills wind turbines sat stationary disturbing only the landscape in the name of progress.

A visitor to the area in 1881 stated that *'Josephville and Caroline are not townships but only railway stations of the skillion description, and are only interesting to the Victorian traveller as being called after a millionaire and his wife who own large tracts of land in the district.'* The critical Victorian visitor was in fact correct since Josephville was named after Joseph Clarke who was a well known farmer in the area. Joseph Clarke was born in Australia in 1835 and bought land in the Lumsden area whilst living at the foot of the hill that gave us such good views over the surrounding countryside, namely Josephville Hill. Joseph Clarke was also a leading figure in the formation of the Waimea Railway Company. Of interest is the fact that a nearby settlement was named after Joseph Clarke's wife, Caroline, thereby providing further proof of their standing within the community. Australian settlement in the area appears to have been quite common since in 1883 the beautifully named newspaper, the Mataura Eagle, stated that *'Mr Mulhare from Victoria has purchased 900 acres freehold and 3,000 acres leasehold on the New Zealand Agricultural Company property in the valley from Josephville to Wantwood.'*

Landscape, Josephville.

43. Ohai

I was apprehensive about visiting our randomly selected locations in Southland, not because I was heading into bandit country where one was likely to be ambushed by gales, torrential rain and even an unseasonable snow flurry driven in by a bitter southerly wind. No, my concern was that this was Southland, the famed land of dairy farmers, flat landscapes, square box road layouts and vistas looking rather too much the same. Surely Ohai would be just one of those places? But no, Ohai was much more. Coal was discovered in the Ohai area during the 1860s close to a stream which flows down a valley north of the current township. However the first commercial mining in the area was not undertaken until 1891. The post office came to Ohai in 1921, the school in 1926, a School of Mines in 1934 and the Mines Rescue Station in 1943. Rivalry on the sporting field with the nearby Nightcaps mining community was said to be notoriously intense, a major understatement if ever there was one.

However what is particularly unusual about Ohai is that in 1916 a decision was made to create a private railway company after the government declined to extend its own railway line from Wairo to the new coalfields at Ohai. Local landowners funded the rail extension through taking out mortgages on their own properties, thereby showing remarkable faith in scheme. The Ohai Railway Board later proved to be the only independent railway company in New Zealand to have run at a profit throughout its existence. Twelve million tons of coal were railed in the first fifty years and in 1992 New Zealand Railways bought the Ohai Railway Board for $1.2 million. This sum of money now forms the basis for the Ohai Railway Fund, a trust that provides grant funding for local community projects.

The Ohai Railway Board offices had always been located in Wairio and I therefore decided to stop by in case any evidence of the original institution remained. And indeed it did. It was a Sunday morning and I had barely finished photographing the picturesque office buildings when a man came out of his cottage, crossed the road, and metaphorically rugby tackled me to the ground. Well not exactly, but Karl Barkley made sure that he showed me everything that he could about the place before I left. And like so many visitors to the area I could well have driven straight past without being aware of the secrets that Wairo had to offer. Karl was an out and out railway enthusiast and had been trying for years, with others, to persuade the authorities that Wairio had a great tourist attraction to offer. Unlocking the main rail shed he showed the most exquisite railway carriage that I have ever seen dating, I assume, from the early 1900s. And in another building a smaller box car stands of a similar design and vintage. Combined with the original Ohai Railway Board offices, complete with boardroom table and photographs, this would be a stop worth making on any heritage trail. Whether or not Wairio becomes a feature on the tourist map any time soon is uncertain but it certainly deserves to be so. And so yet again one of our randomly selected locations had thrown up a very special surprise.

Ohai township itself is a ribbon settlement without any visible centre to the community. In the valley below, mainly hidden from view, a deep coal mine still operates without leaving the characteristic scars on the landscape seen in so many other countries. The mine appeared to be hiding, as if in fear that 'Sea Shepherd' might undergo a metamorphosis into 'Land Shepherd' and environmental activists would enter the township to terrorise the local inhabitants, chain themselves to pit workings, and daub themselves with coal dust for the entertainment of the worlds press and their friends and family back home. But in the meantime Ohai continues its daily task of winning energy from deep underground, a hard and dangerous occupation. And on that note, whilst in Wairio, Karl told me that he had attended the Pike River Memorial service to honour one of the miners who had been killed in the disaster. That man lived in Wairio and travelled weekly to work in Pike River. What a very small world it is.

Ohai Railway Board Carriage, Wairio.

The Coal Mining Town, Ohai.

44. Gummies Bush

Just before Gummies Bush the road crosses the Aparima River along whose banks permanent fishing huts are located at regular intervals. It would appear that these huts belong to individuals since each has its own unique character, perhaps inviting long days spent away from the wife and children just watching the cool clear water flow by. There is no road sign to herald your arrival in Gummies Bush, just a sharp bend in the road close to the former Aparima Dairy Factory. The terminology to describe a number of settlements in this area of Southland is quite common, if not creative, since there is an Otaitai Bush, Gropers Bush, Wrights Bush, Spar Bush and so on. Before European settlement the flat plains all over Southland were covered in bush, predominantly matai, rimu, lowland beech, kanuka and manuka interspersed with tussock grasslands, whilst swamp and bog occupied the low-lying areas. Early settlers named their districts after the particular bush that they cleared and overall there are eighteen Bushes in Southland. Gummies Bush is supposedly named after James Leader, a whaler and later pig farmer, for the simple reason that he had no teeth. Well there you have it.

In 1901 Gummies Bush had just twenty four inhabitants but could nevertheless boast a cooperative dairy factory, a post office, public library, school and a Presbyterian church. In 1904 Alexander Sutherland ran a flax milling operation based at Gummies Bush and which moved to different parts of the district as the flax was cut. Sixteen people were employed in connection with the ten horsepower mobile mill. Flax can still be seen along certain hedge lines, as unattractive to the eye as it ever was. The Aparima Dairy Factory was established in 1901 as a farmers cooperative and by 1903 nearly 100 tons of cheese was being produced. A piggery was attached to the factory to make use of the whey thereby creating an efficient little integrated operation. As elsewhere in New Zealand the dairy factory has now closed and bulk tankers collect milk from individual farms and transport the product to more centralised processing facilities.

At first I was mystified as to why there were so many shelter box hedges in the Gummies Bush area since the district is predominantly dairy and sheep country. I knew that this part of the country was renowned for its wind and rain but surely not strong enough to blow the animals off the landscape. But every so often I noticed ploughed land and the shelter belts must be to stop soil erosion when land preparation for cropping is undertaken, an indication of the fact that this is a fertile area which can adapt its agricultural production as markets change. The land hereabouts is very pleasing to the eye with gently rolling hills and views to the distant coastline. And so that is Gummies Bush, still busily producing food to feed the world.

Fishing Hut, Gummies Bush.

Landscape, Gummies Bush.

45. Isla Bank

The Isla Bank district is named after the River Isla, a tributary of the River Tay in Forfarshire, Scotland. The first permanent settlers from Forfarshire and other parts of Scotland came to the district in the late 1860s and early 1870s. The district, or parts of it, have had other names in its short history: Paulin's Bush, Limestone Plains and Calcium. The last two names were derived from the extensive limestone deposits in the area and Limestone Plains continues to be the name of the parish, whilst the cemetery is still known as Calcium. The name Isla Bank first came into widespread use as the name of the postal district. Confusing or what?

The origins of certain early Isla Bank settlers makes interesting reading. Robert Baird, for example, was born in Kircudbrightshire, Scotland, and landed at Port Chalmers in 1862. He was initially employed breaking-in young horses for ploughing and haulage. After that he worked as a shepherd on an up-country hill station before moving to Limestone Plains. In 1879 he took up 800 acres of leasehold land belonging to the Southland High School Board which was then in tussock grass without fencing or improvement. Over time he brought the land into a good state of cultivation and concentrated on mixed farming, namely both crops and livestock. Alexander McHardy has a slightly different story to tell. He arrived in Lyttelton in 1861 and initially worked as a ploughman before moving to the Otago goldfields were he was initially employed carting products to the diggings. He then combined working on farms and on the goldfields until by 1868 he had accumulated enough funds to buy 119 acres of freehold land at Isla Bank. Ten years later he acquired another 100 acres at the nearby settlement of Drummond. Both Robert Baird and Alexander McHardy demonstrate that in the late 1800s, through hard work and good fortune, a man could progress from being a shepherd to a significant farmer within a very short space of time.

The Isla Bank school was founded in 1873 but changed its site and name more than once before it came to rest at its present location on the crossroads. In 1904 school attendance was recorded at thirty five pupils. In 1883 the unusually named Calcium Mechanics Institute was built on the flat area between St Cuthbert's Church and the school, providing a hall and library for the community until it closed in 1997. Isla Bank's first post office opened in 1874 at the residence of Thomas and Catherine Clark but by 1883 it had shifted to a site at the crossroads before closing down in 1937. As early as 1909 a public telephone and telegram service operated from a small building attached to the Stewart family home until that also closed down in 1967. These facilities demonstrate that even small communities in New Zealand had direct and efficient contacts with the outside world from a very early date.

It seems that virtually every Southland community has its general purpose and livestock transport business and Isla Bank is no exception with Milnes Livestock occupying a key position at the crossroads. The land surrounding Isla Bank is attractive and fertile, not as undulating as Gummies Bush, more a plateau with trees demarcating field boundaries rather than box hedges. On warm sunny days it is certainly a very pleasant place to live.

The neatly tended cemetery is tucked away and a tightly mown grass walkway leads the eye to the war memorial. The impact of the fallen on such small communities must have been earth shattering, indeed heart breaking, leaving wounds which never healed. After struggling for decades to bring the land into fruitfulness, bearing sons and daughters, looking forward to the good life, this happened. Not just here in Isla Bank but across New Zealand and every rural community of the Empire. Eldest sons who were to take on the farm no longer there, sweetheart torn asunder from sweetheart, mothers from sons. And so Isla Bank continues to respect those who left never to return. And long may it be so.

War Memorial, Isla Bank.

Landscape, Isla Bank.

46. Brydone

Driving north along Highway 1 towards Edendale the road suddenly reached the edge of an escarpment and the view and impact reminded me of the beautiful Vale of Evesham in England. The landscape had suddenly changed from a flat productive scene, not at all unattractive, to one that in contrast felt like looking down on the Garden of Eden itself, with hills and mountains as a backdrop. Edendale, on arrival, turned out to be a major Fronterra dairy processing centre but that still did not dull the initial impact of the place. As with so many of our random locations Brydone did not announce itself to us with the formality of signposts. I just happened to momentarily glance to the left and caught a glimpse of the familiar Southland sight of a derelict dairy processing factory which had the name Brydone written clearly on it. Within a short distance we had reached a road junction, the very heart of Brydone itself.

Brydone was originally named Ota Creek but that was before an application was made by the community for the establishment of a post office there in 1906. The name Brydone itself comes from Thomas Brydone, the former Superintendent of the Australian and New Zealand Land Company and the founder of the frozen meat and dairy industry in the country. Thomas Brydone was born in West Linton, Peebleshire, Scotland, and arrived in New Zealand in 1868. In 1882 he personally superintended the loading at Port Chalmers, Dunedin, of the very first chartered vessel to carry frozen mutton from New Zealand to the United Kingdom, as well as supervising the killing and freezing operation. It was also under his direction that the Edendale Dairy Factory was inaugurated and where the first fifty tons of cheese based on the American processing system was manufactured. The wealth of New

Zealand has been built on its agricultural production, particularly meat and dairy products, and the ability to send frozen and chilled products to the other side of the world has been a fundamental component of that success. Thomas Brydone clearly contributed to that success and the people of Brydone no doubt take great pride in their association with his name. Thomas Brydone died in 1904 and that may be why the Ota Creek community, within which he had worked, decided to honour his name after his death.

An impressive war memorial stands next to the Brydone Hall, a facility for the community that had been constructed in 1910 when clearly hope for the future still reigned and the thought of a total war in 1914-1918 had not yet entered the imagination. Behind a high hedge and directly opposite the war memorial stood what seemed to be a private house but on closer inspection it had the distinctive structure of a school building. Whether or not it still acted as a school or had been converted for domestic use was unclear but a group of climbing frames indicated that it might now serve the needs of both. I drove further along a side road in the direction of Pebbly Hill looking for inspiration or perhaps a good photograph, but found none. Returning again to the crossroads I passed the Bryleigh Stud but whether or not a champion had been bred within its confines I could not tell at the time. Beautiful thoroughbreds browsed in the paddocks and it was only later that I learnt that a horse with the name Washington VC, a trotter, resided there and still commanded stud fees of NZ$ 3,000. Washington VC had sired 181 individual winners who between them had accumulated almost NZ$ 9 million in winnings. And so good fortune and fame had come to Brydone in recent times.

The Brydone Dairy Factory Cooperative that I had passed lay derelict as a large milk tanker, no doubt the reason for its demise, sped past on its way to the major processing complex at Edendale. A rusting steam engine took pride of place close to the road boundary but nobody stopped to look. A fading notice on the gate emphatically read 'Keep Out, private property, Southland Steam Club' but the sign looked old and weathered and there was a feeling that the club and even its members were no more. But all was not lost in the Brydone dairy processing world as in September 2010 plans were announced for the establishment of a sheep milking operation to cater for a booming overseas demand for sheep cheese, ice cream and milk powder. If Thomas Brydone had heard about an enterprise milking sheep in Brydone he would have initially fallen over with surprise but would have then quickly picked himself up to supervise the exports.

Yesterday the craggy actor Pete Postlewaite died. He was sixty four. I am sixty two. Ever since 1974 when I first heard Pink Floyd and the particular song 'Time' which includes the words *'Thought I'd something more to say'* and *'You missed the starting gun'* I had been determined not to miss the starting gun. It was just another reason why Sas and I were undertaking this journey.

'Getting sentimental are we Bro?'
'How would you like to join the Southland Steam Club as a prime exhibit next to the steam engine?'
'Lost our sense of humour have we?'

Old Cooperative Factory, Brydone.

Old Farm Buildings, Brydone.

47. Slope Point

The scenery on the journey through the western Catlins, from Fortrose to Slope Point, made it very clear to Sas and I that the trees and shrubs in this southernmost part of New Zealand bend to the will of the winds. It is not a wind that will necessarily break and snap at will, although clearly it can, it is its sheer relentlessness, like a gnawing toothache, that never ceases until total submission from the victim is achieved. Slope Point was not a place for kingly kauri or totara but for fawning species that lay bent and beaten by the westerly wind. And in the absence of trees the land had given way to rich pasture and sheep, as though a spell of sea air had been good for them both. But today, as in recent days, the sun shone brightly on Southland and northern tales about the appalling weather that continually afflicts the south seemed just that, tales.

I left Sas having a doze in the sun whilst I walked down to the headland. I just had to do it since until that moment I had had no idea that it was actually the southernmost point of mainland New Zealand and somehow we just can't resist extremities, can we? You don't get someone climbing Everest just so that they can have their photograph taken one hundred metres from the summit and then just descend. It's not the way that we are built. It is the same with horizons. A signpost informed all who wished to know that due south from Slope Point it was 4,803 kilometres to the South Pole. It is so enticing wanting to know what is just over the horizon and Captain Cook certainly wanted to know, as did his superiors back in England. At the time it was felt that there might be a hidden continent down there which could contain untold riches. He sailed as far south as he could encountering icebergs, severe cold and foul weather before he concluded that no habitable land existed. Today, of course, we know that Antarctica is a continent and that untold riches may indeed lie beneath the frozen ice and snow.

On such a summers day Slope Point was certainly a wonderful sight to see with the deep blue water contrasting so starkly with the white explosions of surf on dark granitic rock. But from now on Sas and I would be heading back north on the final leg of our journey.

'So what was it like?'
'It was really fantastic. A sort of fulfilment of how far we have both come on our travels. Now it's time to think about heading back north again Sas.'
'But what about Black Point Bro? It's only a few kilometres further on and we just have to take a look.'
'But nobody else is going there, so why should we?'
'Exactly my point Bro. That's why we should.'
'No point my arguing then.'
'No point at all.'

It was just a few kilometres of gravel road to Black Point and along the way we glimpsed the outlines of houses hidden in the trees, no doubt seeking protection from the flailing winds. When we arrived at our destination we were the only ones there and the view back to Slope Point was magnificent. It was an ideal place for a picnic and a relaxed hour or two in the sun.

A short distance from Slope Point is Curio Bay and that is where Sas and I spent a couple of nights having a break from our travels. Curio Bay is famous for the Hector's dolphins that seem to have taken a seasonal liking to the place. Usually they just like to bob along without the characteristic extrovert display of leaping and splashing that other dolphins seem to love. But for Sas and my visit they put on a special show and demonstrated their wonderful surfing abilities whilst mere humans in their black wetsuits just stood in the water motionless and admired the real masters of the surf. In the adjacent bay yellow eyed penguins emerged from the sea as if by magic and made their waddling hesitant way to their fast growing chicks hidden in the undergrowth. Young children, away from their 'telescreens', must have left the place with wonder in their hearts.

"Dad, why are we going to Slope Point?"
"Because it's the southernmost point of the South Island son".
"Yes, but why are we going there. Why don't we go to the westernmost point, or the easternmost point, or the south-westernmost point?"
"Mum, are you sure this boy is my son?"
"Yes love, why are we going there?"

Slope Point.

Slope Point.

Masters of the Surf, Curio Bay, Catlins.

48. Quarry Hills

A war memorial and graveyard sit at the road junction which demarcates the centre of the Quarry Hills settlement. The size of the graveyard and the number of gravestones indicate that once Quarry Hills had a larger population but now there is no school, community hall or other indication of their former presence. Nevertheless the photographic record confirms that in 1909 there was a school at Quarry Hills and there we can see Ruby Hansen, Nina Hansen, Letty McMannus, Dolly McDonald, Dorothy Lamb and Lex McLean. Young Lex holds a slate with 'Quarry Hills School' chalked on it but he is much younger than the others, and the spread of ages among the girls is also wide. So perhaps this was it in 1909, a whole school role consisting of just six pupils. And yet that is also the true beauty of the piece, education for all wherever you might live and however many you may be.

One particular gravestone records the deaths of a husband and wife and at the bottom their son Robert Lamb who was killed at Passchendaele. There are many names of Scots origin in the graveyard, Biggar, McLean and so on, and the surrounding landscape has a certain lowland Scottish character to it. A child's toy windmill catches my eye, broken now, beside the grave of a young child of only two and a half years, died 1978. And yet fresh flowers are placed in a vase, and beautifully chosen pebbles from the seashore adorn the spot, perhaps one for each year since her death. Not forgotten, even now. She died in a September but the flowers are only fading now, a remembrance of Christmas past perhaps?

The life or death of rural communities is clearly finely balanced. The Southland Times newspaper reported in September 1901 that *'At a large meeting of settlers at Quarry Hills on Monday night a motion was passed strongly protesting against the action of the Government in proceeding with the survey of another possible route for the extension of the Seaward Bush railway, via Waimahaka Valley, instead of commencing the work of construction via Tokonui as promised some time ago. The farmers of Quarry Hills, at a meeting on Monday night, unanimously decided to form a branch of the New Zealand Farmers Union.'* A new railway line could have significantly boosted the economy of the area but what the final outcome was I do not know. Driving back along the main highway towards Waikawa the Quarry Gallery retains its place opposite a large woolshed. The gallery looks somewhat derelict but through the window I see some paintings and other bric-a-brac, but nobody is at home and I don't think that they have been at home for some considerable time, perhaps years.

It was only much later that I remembered the two young men from our random location of Jacksons who had died in the First World War. One of them, Henry Edward Debenham died at Mesines in France on Friday 12 October 1917, aged 28 years. And now, in far away Quarry Hills, I had found the memorial to young Robert Lamb, killed in action at Passchendaele on the 12 October 1917, aged 26 years. Two young men lost their lives on the other side of the world on the very same day, united in death, their families united in grief.

Landscape, Quarry Hills.

Landscape, Quarry Hills.

49. Finegand

Finegand sounded like it should be the name of a small peaceful Cornish village or a place from the Lord of the Rings trilogy with Gandulf striding along, staff in hand, in the near vicinity. The settlement was named after his Scottish home by John Shaw when he purchased land on the west bank of the Koau River in 1852. A review of the map seemed to confirm that Finegand was just another small rural farming community close to Balclutha but that dot had a major surprise in store for Sas and I. The surrounding landscape consisted of rolling pasture that in places had been cut and baled for winter feed, creating contrasting shapes and colours in the morning sunlight. A branch of the ubiquitous Clutha River flowed past close by, a friend that we had met on a number of previous occasions on our journey, now just a handful of kilometres from freedom and the sea. The Finegand bowling club stands adjacent to the centre of the community behind high protective walls of green, the floodlights emphasising the feeling of an internment camp rather than a place where heavy bowl clicks on heavy bowl on a pristine green. And at the nearby road junction a faded billboard advertised 'Country Gifts, Collectibles and Antiques', just forty metres along the road, but a closed sign hung beneath as probably it had done for many years, undisturbed, apart by the wind.

The surprise that Finegand had in store for us was that it is actually the location of a major meat freezing works where all those cuddly lambs and beef cattle go to meet their maker far earlier than they had anticipated. For that is the stark reality since if you happen to enjoy eating your Sunday roast then death must come at some time on the journey to your plate. The Finegand works has been in existence for one hundred years and in early 2011 the demise of the one hundred millionth lamb to be slaughtered there since its opening was ritually celebrated. Meat workers are a tough bunch and it is hard physical work handling heavy carcasses on the equivalent of a production line. It is also dangerous work with razor sharp knives and powered chain saws all trying to keep up with strict piecework schedules. One thousand people work at Finegand and therefore it is by far the most important employer in the region. However the typical killing season only lasts from November until July and as many as two hundred workers find it difficult to find additional employment during the long off-season. And always, it seems, there is the threat of closure as global competition becomes more intense, if not here then at the freezing works in other parts of the country.

Take away one thousand jobs from this area and you destroy it as effectively and as precisely as an atomic bomb, and all due to the great god demand and supply. And so in the cyclical bad times the experts always look for ways to cut costs and the place that they look is at Gary, Mike and John. Better a few jobs lost than all, isn't that so? And of course Marvin can do the work of those three but it just so happens that Marvin is a robot. It is the shareholders dream, a plant completely manned by robots each working without a tea break, and without a human being in sight to complicate the issue. And no doubt, in some far off laboratory in Japan, the experts are working on Rover the robotic sheepdog to partner Phil the robotic shepherd who can summon at will Sam the GPS driven livestock truck. And in the golden future one thousand former workers and their families will look mournfully over the security patrolled fence and admire the marvels of technology before shuffling back to their metaphorical soup kitchen in Balclutha. Sas and I take the Freezing Works Road which appropriately leads away from the factory and soon we are in rolling hills of clover and newly ploughed arable land. We stop for a while to admire the view but skylarks start complaining loudly about our presence and therefore we depart in haste.

Welcome to Finegand.

Landscape, Finegand.

50. Pyramid

It was a pretty miserable day as we approached Pyramid and the rain was relentless, the worst of the whole trip. On the original map used for the random selection process Pyramid was marked as a settlement but on our larger scale 2010 map it was simply marked as a hill. The attractively named Pyramid Fingerpost Road signpost helpfully pointed us in the right direction but as we approached it, the hill after which the location Pyramid was named, looked nothing like a pyramid at all, at least not to us. On the road from Gore a number of other hills had certainly made passable pyramids, or at least cones, and even an alternative summit close to the hill that we were looking at had the features required. But not the one actually named Pyramid. Perhaps the original prospector, settler or surveyor was drunk at the time and in this driving rain I certainly sympathised.

The Mataura River flows beneath Pyramid and I left Sas to take a photograph of a particularly attractive white painted wooden bridge which seemed to be of an ancient vintage. Sheep covered a nearby hillside in profusion, like patches of snow after an unseasonable springtime storm. It was only after taking the photograph that I looked down and noticed a stout wooden cross that was almost hidden from view by long grass. Hung over the white cross were a pair of unusual leather shoes, more like overshoes, of a very old design. They were not the shoes of a child but seemed more like those of an old person, perhaps suffering from gout. The shoe design was almost medieval in its simplicity and crude cut. They must surely have belonged to the person who died? There was no indication of who that person may have been or how they might have died, a car crash or suicide, perhaps. It was a sad but wonderful mystery that Pyramid had presented to us when the potential of the place for surprise had seemed so limited.

The mystery of the Pyramid cross would not leave my mind and later research seems to have provided a partial answer. It appears that at about 10.45 pm on the 4th April 2004 a Jeep four wheel drive vehicle crashed through the wooden barriers of the bridge and landed on its roof in the river. The alarm was raised by a passing motorist who noticed the damaged railings at about 11.45 pm that same night. The next day the local police constable and thirty volunteers searched the surrounding area for the missing driver who was known to live in the nearby Riversdale settlement. An unsuccessful search was also carried out on the next day, including two jet boats, but still no sign of the victim could be found. And that is all that I know since no further record of the incident could be found, and so it is still a mystery. In March 2009 the, by now, senior police constable died of a heart attack whilst competing in a mountain bike race from Wanaka to Arrowtown. He was a former New Zealand track cyclist who had competed in the 1974 Commonwealth Games. Over 1,000 people attended his funeral illustrating the respect with which he was held within Riversdale and the surrounding community. Small community, big hearts.

We finally drove on towards our night stop at distant Alexandra but took the back road via Otama, Chatton, Waikaka, Kelso and Heriot. The farmland in the area was superb and it made me reflect on how few people in the country are responsible for producing off the land and that the land could have no better caretakers than themselves. Most people do not take the opportunity to visit the back roads of New Zealand, keeping as they do to the main highways, but if they did they would be truly proud of their farming community.

Bridge over the Mataura River, Pyramid.

Memorial Mystery, Pyramid.

51. Ettrick

Ettrick is located on a highway that is so straight that a jumbo jet could land there if a few telegraph poles were to be strategically removed. The highway is one of the major routes between the city of Dunedin and the Central Lakes area but the volume of traffic passing through was still a surprise. Drivers slowed down when they arrived but only because of the speed limit and not for any other reason that I could tell. Fruit packing and cool storage sheds stand within the town boundary and surrounding orchards state that they are proud to supply ENZA, formerly the New Zealand Apple and Pear Marketing Board, but then who else could they supply? What ENZA has done for Ettrick in return was rather unclear because the overall feeling of the place was of decline and decay. Perhaps ENZA had supplied the smart new Ettrick signboard on the side of the highway since that seemed to be the only new structure of note.

Ettrick's problem is that apple production is a continual battle for survival with new varieties being developed year after year with the objective of tempting the overseas buyer with look, taste and texture. Braeburn, Royal Gala, Fuji, Pacific Rose, Pacific Queen, Pacific Beauty, Jazz, and the new kid on the block, Envy, all compete for the housewife's dollar, pound and yen. And in the apple world all is not fair in love and war since the country's arch enemy at cricket, rugby, football and particularly netball, Australia, had closed access to New Zealand apples for eighty nine years. The World Trade Organisation finally ruled in 2010 that Australia had to open up its market to it's Tasman Sea neighbour but a major Ettrick personality and fruit producer, Con van der Voort, recognised that access could still be made difficult but at least it was a start.

'So Bro, I guess that you're not that keen on Ettrick?'
'It's just that I think that they should smarten the place up a bit and add one or two attractive signboards to highlight the places to visit in Ettrick. Just like Houhora should.'
'Hou what?'
'Very amusing Sas but I'm not falling for that one'
'Pity. I thought that you would.'

Just a few kilometres south of Ettrick, close to Rigney, can be found the location of an event that is well known in New Zealand folklore. In 1864 a local gold miner, William Rigney, came across a small, shivering dog that was keeping guard over the body of a dead man near what was then called Horseshoe Bend Diggings. It was subsequently determined that the young man had died from drowning or exposure but his identity remained unknown. With nobody to claim the body William Rigney asked for permission to bury him near to where the man had been found. With no known name to place on the man's tombstone, Rigney carved a wooden tombstone with the words *'Somebody's Darling Lies Buried Here'*. When Rigney himself died in 1912 he stipulated in his will that he was to be buried alongside Somebody's Darling. His grave reads *'Here Lies William Rigney, The Man Who Buried Somebody's Darling'*.

Welcome to Ettrick.

Cottage, Ettrick.

52. Butchers Gully

The landscape on the way from Alexandra to Butcher's Gully was dry and dramatic with distinctively shaped rocks of huge proportions laid out as if for effect. Much of this land is now for sale as 'lifestyle' properties but why anyone would choose to live permanently in such a barren landscape I have no idea. The views to the highlands would be interesting for a day but for a lifetime, however short, no way. Water is in short supply here in the hills since the appropriately named Last Chance Water Company controls the Butcher's Gully lake and any idea of creating a boutique vintage wine to impress your friends would be out of the question.

Gold was discovered in Butcher's Gully in 1862. For a short time it was known as 'Hill's Gully' after it's discoverer, and later as 'Londonderry' but these names did not endure for long. By 1863 the gully was commonly referred to as 'Butcher's Gully' yet no one knows exactly why. One story refers to a hotel and butcher's shop in the gully owned by Charles Nieper and Henry Wilkinson around 1865. An alternative story tells of a herd of cattle stampeding whilst being driven through the steep gullies that now lie beneath the lake created by Butcher's Dam. Several cattle reportedly fell over the cliffs and died after which the carcasses were butchered and the meat distributed amongst the miners who witnessed or heard the carnage.

An interesting story relating to Butchers Gully is told by members of the Theyers Family History Society:

'The storekeeper was always required to be keen, and in the early days had to do his own debt collecting. William Theyers, of Manuherikia, was a generous, kindly man, always prepared to allow long credit in a deserving case, but with a horror of the man who sneaks away and tries to avoid payment of a just debt. He had a very original way of treating such.

About 1865 a great exodus of diggers took place from Otago to the West Coast, and Theyers found that quite a number of men who owed him money had slipped away without saying good-bye. They all took money with them for expenses, and, no doubt, intended to send the storekeeper his money by and by if they got a good claim, but if not ----. This way of doing business did not appeal to Theyers. Being at that time a very powerful and active young man, he made it a practice to ride after every departing digger who owed him money and thrash the man until he paid up, and in time this practice made him a terror to defaulters. One morning he heard that a big Irishman from the Old Man Range was removing himself, and, getting on his horse, picked up Charlie Nieper, who had a hotel and butcher's shop at Butcher's Gully, and with him pushed on towards the Fourteen Mile Beach. When they got near the river they came up on their man, and the following dialogue took place:

Theyers (speaking as usual in a slow, deliberate voice, nodding his head with each phrase): 'Hey! Are you going to pay me?'
Digger: 'You can go to hell! You will get no money from me.'
Thcyers: 'We'll see about that. Hold my horse, Charlie.'
Then followed a rough and tumble encounter with heavy blows and an occasional remark from Theyers.
'When you have had enough and are going to pay me, I'll stop.'
At last the digger said, 'But you can't give me a receipt.'
'Yes, I can', said Theyers, and produced pen, ink, stamp and paper, when the hard-earned money was at last paid over.
Then said Theyers, 'I'll hold the horses, Charlie, and you get your account.'

The big man again refused to pay, and Nieper threw off his coat and tried a round, but, being a small, light man, found he had no hope of success.
Theyers: 'Come and hold the horses again, Charlie, and I'll quieten him for you.'
Digger: 'Oh! If I have to fight you again, I may as well pay him too.'

The moral effect of an event of this sort must have been great, and very few debtors would run the risk of such an encounter. Theyers was a highly successful storekeeper and became one of the chief pillars of Alexandra and its institutions.'

Butcher's Dam, which was built in the 1930s, is itself an example of the extreme need for water resources in a dry environment that makes it the equivalent of liquid gold. A photograph of the original Butcher's Gully hotel was shown on the information board but now it lies several metres below the waters surface and so Sas and I were not able to visit the original settlement of Butcher's Gully, and neither will anyone else. Why a hotel should have been built in this particular location in the first place is difficult to understand at this distance in time because Alexandra lies close by in the well watered valley of the swift flowing Clutha River. But then Butchers Gully endured for many years and the logic at the time must therefore have been sound.

Former Butchers Gully Hotel.

Butchers Gully Dam.

53. Bortons

Getting to Bortons from Alexandra was never going to be easy since the Hawkdun Range, Ida Range and Kakanui Mountains create a barrier to any direct route. I was happy to take the long way around via Cromwell, Tarras and Omarama before heading down Highway 83 towards Oamaru. However Sas would hear none of it and when she spotted a more direct route via Highway 85, Naseby and Danseys Pass there was no stopping her, particularly as it included about forty kilometres of gravel road. And as usual she was right since we made the journey in clear blue skies, high up in the mountains with beautiful views in every direction and all of it to ourselves.

Except that was for a police wagon travelling in the opposite direction around one of the narrow hairpin bends with a sheer drop to the left. Fortunately Sas was behaving herself at the time and on the correct side of the track. Later on that day we read that a father and his two young daughters had spent the previous night in their car after they got lost looking for the route over Danseys Pass and perhaps that was why the policeman was heading for the hills. It didn't surprise us because as usual there were very few signposts on the route and we just had to rely on our map and a good sense of direction. I believe that his estranged wife was later reported to have been very upset by his temporary disappearance but all the poor joker was trying to do was to show his children the beauty of their own country rather than the easy option of dumping them down in front of a 'telescreen'. No doubt he will be up in front of the social workers where he will be punished rather than praised for his actions.

On the way to the actual pass we drove through the pretty settlement of Naseby and later on we came across the Danseys Pass Coach Inn which was built in 1862. The Inn was located directly besides the historic settlement of Kyeburn Diggings and at one time a gold prospecting community of 2,000 people lived in the area.

Bortons itself lies in the wide Waitaki River valley and although it is clearly marked as an actual place on our map we never did positively identify its exact location. Bortons was named after John Borton who was a surveyor and engineer who settled in the district in 1854. Bortons is certainly located on well tended and rich agricultural land just above the flood plain of the river. However it seems that Bortons major role is in the collection of irrigation water from the Waitaki River for the North Otago Irrigation Scheme. North Otago is a notoriously dry district and frequent droughts make profitable farming without irrigation very difficult. Water is therefore pumped from the river at Bortons into enormous holding ponds from where it is gradually released into the irrigation scheme throughout the summer. At present 10,000 hectares are irrigated but plans are in hand to extend the irrigated area to 40,000 hectares. The attraction of the scheme is that hydroelectric power is generated from the Otago rivers further upstream and a proportion of that power is then used to power the pumps at Bortons to lift the water into the holding reservoirs. In an age of rising populations and increasing concerns about global food supply the development does look to serve a useful purpose.

Apart from a charming little cottage there were no other defining features or points of interest about Bortons. Put a country lane through this landscape and it would have been a beautiful area but as soon as a main highway passes through the tranquility is simply destroyed by the regular passing of high speed traffic. However on the positive side Sas and I would never have had any reason to travel over the Danseys Pass road without our random selection of Bortons and for that we had to be truly grateful.

On the road to Danseys Pass.

Landscape, Danseys Pass.

Bortons.

54. Woodbury

As we drove towards Woodbury from Geraldine my attention was immediately drawn to a signpost pointing to the Woodbury Cemetery. It is a peaceful burying ground enclosed by giant fir trees, some of which resembled redwoods to my inexpert eye. It is a wonderful last resting place where local people can be remembered. One of the gravestones read *'Died doing what he loved best'* and I could not guess what that might be, possibly skiiing or making love, but then in the top corner was the engraving of a car. It immediately made me think of an alternative inscription that may have been more apt since this was the last resting place of a young man although, on reflection, the thought was unkind since I did not know the circumstances that led to his death. It's just that too many Kiwis waste their young lives in that way, and sometimes take the lives of innocents along with them whether they be passengers, pedestrians or other road users. Another gravestone remembers their young son who *'Died in the mountains'* but somehow a similar sentiment did not seem to apply and yet perhaps it should. But how could anyone living so close to the mountains resist their draw.

We drove a little further on and Woodbury turned out to be a much more substantial settlement than we had been used to lately. 'The great little rural school' was written on the Woodbury School sign and I'm sure that the words are true. At the main crossroads the Eleanor Howard Tripp Memorial Library stands, named after one of Woodbury's illustrious former residents. The library was open but there was no one present and, refreshingly, trust was clearly in play in Woodbury. One room consisted of a small library and the other had a wonderful collection of memorabilia relating to Woodbury. I learnt that the Woodbury township was first established in 1853 when two men named Muter and Francis took out a license to occupy parts of Raukapuka Station. The settlement was at that time known as Waihi Bush and it was not until 1879 that it was renamed Woodbury. Woodbury is certainly a well ordered and affluent community and a feeling was gained that the Tripp family held some sway over it, just like the country squire holds over certain English villages, even to this day.

We left the crossroads in search of the church and on turning a corner I was transported thousands of kilometres back to the heart of England, for there in front of me was a typical English country church, St Thomas. We returned to the crossroads since the church was locked and true believers would therefore just have to be patient. Opposite the library was a building that clearly used to be a shop of some kind and for some reason it looked familiar. I looked again at the library and then at the shop and I knew for sure where I had seen them both before. It was when I was undertaking research in England using the internet and the photographic image that I had seen of Woodbury made me wonder what the impressive memorial was that stood in front of what I now knew to be the library. But somehow the internet images that I had seen seemed cold and sterile compared to the actuality of being in the place, hearing the sounds, feeling the breeze, and inhaling the soft scents on the wind.

Memorial Library, Woodbury.

Memorial Library, Woodbury.

55. Ruapuna

The grain silos along the road indicated that Ruapuna was located in an important cereal production area. However the grain production was clearly not won easily from the land here as evidenced by the huge piles of boulders which were liberally concentrated in piles throughout many of the fields. Originally the boulders must have been scattered across the whole landscape and each one had to be lifted and moved to make the land suitable for agriculture. Whether or not the majority of this work was undertaken by hand by the original settlers or by specialised machinery at a later date I could not tell. It simply reinforced the view that one should not take for granted the wonderful agricultural land which is now spread out before our eyes in this country, and indeed in any country.

The stones had not been entirely discarded since at the central crossroads sat All Saints church and it appeared to have been constructed of the very same boulders. Unfortunately the church did not have the grace and beauty of a typical New Zealand wooden church but I guess that what it looked like missed the main point of its existence. We found out that services were every second Sunday of every odd month and every fifth Sunday and it might still take us a few more months to work that out. On the opposite side of the crossroads stood the Ruapuna memorial gates, relics of an age when they actually signified the entrance to something. Now they sat isolated, guarding nothing but an open plan stretch of grass where perhaps the former Ruapuna Hall once stood. But somewhere about these parts Ruapuna had it's very own horse whisperer who would take on your problem horse and make it follow your every command. According to the newspapers it seems that he was not averse to the rodeo and had had to crawl out from under the bucking broncos on more than one occasion.

'So that's it then Bro?'
'What do you mean, that's it?'
'Well, that's all you have to say about poor little Ruapuna.'
'Well what more can I say? It's just a very pleasant place with crops and pasture to the horizon, and the mountains as a backdrop. I just haven't found anything unusual or particularly exciting about the place.'
'No offence, just asking.'

Landscape, Ruapuna.

All Saints Church, Ruapuna.

56. Hakatere

The drive along the Inland Scenic Route is always a pleasure when compared to Highway 1. Hakatere lies quite a few kilometres beyond the Mount Somers turnoff and the scenery along the way was so beautiful that frequent stops were required to take photographs of what appeared to be increasingly wonderful sights on a blue sky day. Hakatere itself was at the end of the sealed road and the centre of interest was clearly the buildings of the old Hakatere Station. They were extremely attractive and made the journey worthwhile since they had so much historic character. There were newer farm buildings nearby but it was difficult to identify any individual homes since they were hidden from view by tall pine trees. As far as I could see there was no school, memorial hall, graveyard or any other evidence of extensive settlement in Hakatere.

Sas once again noticed two gravel roads of interest leading off into the far distance and we took the Mount Potts road since it seemed to offer the possibility of mountain views. Soon we came upon the Lake Clearwater recreation area which consisted of holiday bachs of character and interest. It had the feel of a religious cult of some kind but the number of boat trailers indicated that it was a different type of cult which frequented the place and in this holiday season it was certainly very popular. All the time I was thinking that we had seen quite enough but Sas is always wondering what lies beyond the next bend and we therefore just had to continue on along the rough gravel road.

There is only one word to describe the sight which met our eyes as we passed by Harpers Knob and that word is Paradise. It was as if we had suddenly entered a magical, mystical, hidden kingdom. The hills that had enclosed us suddenly opened up to give a panoramic vista of unrivalled beauty. I can honestly say that it was the most beautiful sight that I had ever seen in New Zealand and I have certainly seen many amazing sights in my time. A broad valley floor opened up to both left and right and in the distance the Havelock River led the eye to the sheer mountain peaks of the Southern Alps with the remnants of winter snow on their flanks. The map identified a number of mountaineering and tramping huts with intriguing names such as Mistake Flats Hut, Finlay Face Hut and Curtis Memorial Hut. Interesting, perhaps tragic stories certainly lay behind those names. And as I stood there another name for the area came to mind and that was simply, Shangri-La. I felt for a moment that we would never be allowed to leave the area since we had seen the hidden secret and it was a secret that could not be passed on to other mortals. We turned around with heavy hearts for however many times we return we will never be able to capture the magic of that moment again.

Old Hakatere Station, Hakatere.

Lake Clearwater Camp, near Hakatere.

Shangri-La, Mount Potts Road, beyond Hakatere.

57. Hororata

A signpost on the Inland Scenic Route pointed the way to Hororata when we were still twenty kilometres distant and for one of our random locations to be actually identified by a signpost was quite a novelty. On the outskirts of Hororata itself an attractive billboard invited us to take a coffee at the local cafe and that was just what I needed to raise my spirits. Unfortunately the cafe was closed, hopefully because it was a Sunday, though there was a distinct air of past glories and a sense of slow decay about Hororata. The Domain and Ornamental Lake, established 1877, beckoned us and proudly stated that it had all the facilities that a small community could want including four tennis courts, a children's playground, scout den and even a race course. The public toilets, of breeze block construction, had an impressive mural painted on the back wall but some of the illustrated buildings didn't seem to relate to Hororata itself but to a different place, which seemed odd.

Someone was certainly big on the erection of health and safety signs within the domain since a very large number were nailed to the trunks of the pine trees, and one in particular caught my eye, *'Beware. Watch for Horses'*. There were so many different signs that it was therefore surprising that there wasn't one with the warning to all and sundry, *'Beware. Watch for Trees'*. The attractive wooden tennis club hut sat peacefully in the shade by the very courts where it had long ago witnessed Drew beat Michael in that cracking 1937 singles final. But now two of the four courts had flourishing weeds and it was clear that before long they would take over the whole area through a lack of interest. The impressive Ornamental Lake to the rear of the tennis hut was no longer ornamental since the water and care lavished on it long ago had drained away. I thought that perhaps a neutron bomb had fallen on Hororata without anyone outside noticing since there was no children's laughter on the swings, no gossip being exchanged, the place devoid of human presence on a beautiful blue sky sunny day. Perhaps I should not have been surprised, since as Joni Mitchell sang long ago, *'Everything comes and goes'* and that is just what is happening to so many of the rural settlements that Sas and I have visited. *'Sometimes you're thinking you've finally got it made, bad news comes knocking on your garden gate'*.

We drove further beyond the domain and came across a sweet little wooden church where a baptism seemed to be in progress. So some people did survive the Hororata bomb then. A high security fence around the adjacent St John's Church seemed on first impressions to have been built to keep out believers and unbelievers alike, without distinction, but then it suddenly dawned on us what this was all about. A bomb had certainly hit Hororata but it was an earthquake that had caused the stone belfry of St John's Church to collapse in on itself. And the road sign revealed to us that Darfield, the epicentre of the September 2010 quake, was only eighteen kilometres away. I began to feel embarrassed, even ashamed, about the comments that I had made about the slow decay of Hororata. But on reflection the two events were not related, were they, even though they were just as real. One was the result of the inevitable slow decline of a rural community in the modern age and the other was a brutal force that had struck without warning early one September morning. The church will no doubt be rebuilt but whether or not Hororata will thrive again was difficult to tell. It certainly can if the people of Hororata will it to be so.

The Domain, Hororata.

Earthquake Damage, Hororata.

58. Diamond Harbour

Diamond Harbour lies on the Banks Peninsula directly opposite the major port of Lyttleton where oil tankers, container ships and cruise liners regularly arrive from all corners of the world. I parked Sas at the top of the hill next to the County Stores, much to her annoyance, since there was a definite risk of driving down to the constricted wharf area and not finding a parking space. I was confident about my decision since there was an obvious pathway heading straight downwards to the bay. It was a foolproof scheme. I set off under the shade of the pine trees but unfortunately my marvellous plan ultimately led me to a small bay separated from the actual Diamond Harbour wharf by about four hundred metres of large rocks set right up against the steep slope of the hillside, and no clear pathway between the two. This was indeed a worthy challenge for a juvenile mind and the scramble up, over and around the giant rocks was certainly rewarding. There was absolutely no way I was going to retreat defeated up that path again with Sas looking on. Along the shoreline I passed two Maori lads swimming in the ice cold water searching for their dinner but they told me that so far they hadn't had any luck.

The actual location of the wharf and yacht moorings was certainly very pleasing to the eye and a million miles from the sprawling city of Christchurch just beyond the far hill. Diamond Harbour clearly had a small but thriving community and it was therefore an attractive place to live. A frequent passenger ferry provides transport to work for those who wished to do so and to the other facilities that are to be found in Lyttleton and Christchurch beyond. But the civilised life itself remains in Diamond Harbour.

Until very recently a focal point of the settlement used to be Godley House and a billboard by the wharf proudly declared that it offered accommodation, a restaurant, a bar and a cafe. Unfortunately, being of brick construction, the building was seriously damaged by the 4th September 2010 earthquake and the property had been closed for repair, or perhaps demolition, ever since. Godley House was built in 1880 by one Harvey Hawkins as a family home. He was one of Lyttelton's leading citizens and made his living as a ship chandler, ironmonger and speculator. The land that Godley House was built on had been purchased by Harvey Hawkins from Mark Stoddart. However the good times did not last long for Harvey and by 1894 he had been declared bankrupt and when the property went on the market it did not attract a single bid. So by default the house reverted to the Stoddart family. The Stoddarts subsequently lived there until 1913 when their own cottage and the house were both sold to Lyttelton Council. It was the Council that subsequently named the mansion after John Robert Godley, a pioneer settler in the area. When the earthquake struck in 2010 the five occupants of Godley House were asleep upstairs and they were therefore lucky to escape with their lives. Apart from Godley House there were no obvious signs of earthquake damage in the Diamond Bay area that we could see but no doubt every structure had received its own fair share of damage.

We were just about to drive away when a glance to my left revealed a quaint little cottage in a sun drenched clearing which also housed the rugby, cricket and bowls clubs. On closer inspection the sign at the Diamond Harbour Rugby Club entrance proudly declared that it was the first 'smoke free' club in New Zealand but it will be a very sad day when the first New Zealand rugby club declares itself to be the first 'beer free' club. The cottage itself was transported in prefabricated form from Australia to its present location in 1862 as the home of Mark Pringle Stoddart. Mark Stoddart was born in Edinburgh in 1819, the son of an admiral in the British navy. After farming in Australia for a short period of time he travelled to New Zealand in 1852 where he soon became the owner of fifty five acres of land in the place that he himself named Diamond Harbour, reportedly after seeing its waters glistening in the sun. Stoddart's Cottage was also the birthplace of one of New Zealand's foremost artists, Margaret Stoddart. Margaret Olrog Stoddart was born in Stoddart's Cottage on the 3rd October 1865. At the age of 17 Margaret enrolled at the Canterbury College School in Christchurch to study art and it was during this period that her interest in floral subjects began. After the death of her father in 1885 Margaret moved back to Diamond Harbour to live with her mother and sisters in the mansion that was to become Godley House. By the time that she died in 1934 she had become one of New Zealand's most popular artists and had exhibited worldwide.

The story of Diamond Harbour seems to revolve around earthquakes since it was the financial earthquake which led to Harvey Hawkins having to dispose of what must have been his pride and joy, Godley House, for which he received not a single penny. And 115 years later the present owners saw their successful business destroyed in a few minutes by the power of nature. And yet somehow I believe that both families had to bear the shock and as the song goes, *'Pick yourself up, dust yourself off and start all over again'*.

Diamond Harbour.

Stoddart's Cottage, Diamond Harbour.

59. Spotswood

Spotswood lies close to the magnificent Waiau River where both the road and railway bridges are remarkable for their length. The settlement of Spotswood itself seems to be centred on the corrugated iron construction of the Spotswood Hall where a memorial to those who were lost in the 1914-1918 war is also located. The inscription indicates that the small communities of Spotswood, and nearby Leominster, paid an excessively high personal price since fourteen names are listed. Unusually there were no names engraved on the memorial for the Second World War. Perhaps they were just lucky or perhaps the people of Spotswood felt that they had already paid too high a price once before and simply said *'Stuff it, we won't serve'*. But I am sure that they served, once more rallying to the cause. The grass around the hall was neatly mown and two tennis courts at the rear looked as if they might still be in use since the nets were taut and ready for play.

On the other side of the main road a sign seemed to raise the possibility that Spotswood may once have had its own railway station but a dual track is all that remains for trains passing north and south. Further along the line an attractive wooden structure stands besides the track. It is used by the train drivers to change the points for the passing trains, and perhaps where they can also have a quick chat about family and friends. The name Spots Wood is painted on the side of the structure and I can only assume that this was a simple mistake or perhaps somebody was having their own little private joke at the expense of the community. The land about is parched and dry except where irrigation sprinklers project their liquid gold onto the welcoming soil. But summer drought in this area is just an annual event and not of any particular surprise to the local farming community. Surrounding Spotswood, like Indians circling a wagon train, are Mount Emily, Mount Ward and the intriguingly named The Wart, also Dead Mans Hill and further away Mount Beautiful. And as with so many rural communities in New Zealand they love their horse racing in Spotswood and a full size racecourse with stands was laid out many years ago, but there is no indication that another race will ever be run.

It's hard to believe by looking at the place that Spotswood once had a school of its own, established in 1895, and that by 1902 the average attendance was an impressive forty one. Sas and I could see no sign of the building itself, unless perhaps it was one and the same as the hall. It would make sense. The records state that surrounding the school was an area of two acres whilst the teachers accommodation stretched to five rooms, a large investment in the benefits of education by any standard. The rural school in New Zealand clearly helped to establish the firm foundations for the rapid economic development of the country as a whole. The simple ability to read, write and add up helped thousands to make their way in the world but unfortunately the selfsame schools are rapidly becoming historic relics on their way to joining the cooperative dairy factory, communal hall and war memorial as crumbling memories of another age. Now rural children are being transported long distances to larger more impersonal centres of education where they can achieve 'universal standards' and along that path something fundamental has been lost. One can only hope that in the age of the internet geographical distance will no longer be the handicap that it is today and once again more people will have the opportunity to live, work and play in the countryside.

Old Railway Sign, Spotswood.

Railway Control, Spotswood.

60. Swyncombe

And so at long last Sas and I had arrived in the general vicinity of our final destination, Swyncombe, just a dolphin's leap from the magnificent Kaikoura coastline. It had been a journey that had taken us from the virtual north to the virtual south of the country and into areas that we would never have ventured had it not been for the random loss of sanity that led to the birth of this journey. In comparison to a number of our previous visits locating Swyncombe should have been a very simple matter since in the 2007 edition of the New Zealand Globetrotter map (Scale 1: 900,000), the very one that I had used to select the sixty random locations in the first place, it was clearly marked as a small settlement just a short distance from Highway 70 and towards the foot of the Seaward Kaikoura Range. What could be easier? However we have a problem Houston since on the far more detailed 2010 edition of the AA New Zealand map (Scale 1: 300,000) the settlement of Swyncombe no longer existed, completely eradicated from existence in true Orwellian fashion. All that was now shown was the same side road and a hill nearby named Swyncombe. In so many ways Swyncombe was therefore an entirely appropriate place to end our journey since it was representative of so many of the rural places that we had previously visited, emphasising their slow painful journey into obscurity until finally their very existence will no longer be recorded or remembered, like the dead without gravestones to mark their passing.

We drove past a new 'lifestyle' development where ill-matched houses sat on parched land amid eddies of rising dust. Just over the horizon, yes just over there, is the sea that the owners had hoped to be close to but could not quite afford. Further along the road more houses were hidden behind high hedges but we still could not locate the road that should have led to the, by now, mythical Swyncombe. Confused, we took photographs of the general landscape since that seemed to be all that we would find. It was so very disappointing not being able to locate our final random location, a sad end to a great adventure.

We returned from our search of the surrounding area and parked at what appeared to be the entrance to a private house hidden by trees. The variety of trees planted at the entrance seemed to hint at the former glories of the old Swyncombe, rather like the long tree-lined driveway leading up to Mandalay in Daphne du Maurier's book Rebecca. As usual Sas was keen to explore the gravel road but I didn't want to intrude on someone's private property which surely lay just a few metres beyond the trees where we sat. It would have been just too embarrassing, sweeping up to the front of their house within seconds and covering the occupants and their leisurely lunch with dust. But just then I looked more closely at the white painted wooden post box and what I had initially thought to be the faded name of the owners of the property turned out on closer inspection to read Swyncombe. Barely legible, but the letters definitely spelt out Swyncombe. Without waiting for my decision Sas charged through the tree lined entrance and instead of the immediate sight of a house and its shocked owners a long straight gravel road opened out before us and led onwards into the distance and towards the hills.

The history books tell us that Swyncombe was originally an extensive property of 9,500 acres and that it was first occupied in 1854 by Captain George Rock Keene. In fact Swyncombe has an infamous place in New Zealand history since the Keene family were probably the first to introduce rabbits into the Kaikoura region in the 1860s for sport and as a source of food. In fact in April 1869 the Governor, George Bowen, asked the Keenes for a supply of silver grey rabbits to serve up to Prince Alfred who was at that time touring the country. In the six months leading up to October 1869 a total of 10,000 rabbits were trapped at Swyncombe. Another report states that in 1875 a total of 120,000 rabbit skins were shipped out of Kaikoura. Despite the huge number of rabbits caught they ultimately depleted the pasture and eroded the hillsides of Swyncombe forcing the Keenes to walk off the property in 1882. In just a few years an ecological disaster had occurred.

Following the Keenes departure the property was sold to William Derisley Wood. William Wood was born on the 17 December 1824 in Great Blakenham, Suffolk, where his father was a flour miller. William initially settled in Christchurch but at a later stage returned to England where he bought a prefabricated windmill that he shipped back to Christchurch for assembly and flour milling subsequently commenced in earnest on the 18 August 1856. William later built a number of water powered and electrically powered mills and at the time of his death he left what was then the considerable fortune of 87,185 pounds. William had the capital to erect rabbit fences and brought a large area of Swyncombe back into full production through improved farming practices. Nevertheless Swyncombe still offers a vivid illustration of what happens when an alien species is introduced into a country without any control. It is a problem that has afflicted New Zealand in the past and that will continue to do so in the future. The isolation of New Zealand helped protect its indigenous species for tens of thousands of years until the first human settlement of the country. The rapid extinction of the moa and many other native fauna and flora could not be avoided in the past and today the threat is even greater as global trade and travel easily penetrate existing phytosanitary barriers. So when you look on the place that was once named Swyncombe take a good look at the landscape that is New Zealand, for it is under threat as never before. And to be quite honest there is absolutely nothing we can do about it, whatever anybody might say.

Swyncombe, Faded History.

Beef Cattle, Swyncombe.

Napier: The journey ends

'So that's it then Sas. We did it. We knocked the bastard off as Sir Ed famously said when he conquered Everest.'

'Look Bro, we've just returned from a leisurely trip around New Zealand. It hardly compares. And please watch your language. You know that I don't like it.'

'But Sir Ed.....'

'No buts Bro.'

'Well anyway we covered all of our sixty random locations, didn't miss a single one, and arrived home safely. Apart from your little illness just south of Warkworth after only five days. Man I thought that you were a goner.'

'It was just a bit of hay fever. It was never anything to worry about.'

'It was your ignition. You were dead as a dodo until that nice AA ambulance carried you into Dr Wilmots in Whitaker Road.'

'I'd have been alright after a little rest.'

'Anyway Sas, thanks for everything. I could never have done it without you. You're an absolute star.'

'Well thanks Bro. I have to say that I really enjoyed it myself. Sad that it's over really. So I guess that now you're going to dump me back at Prebensen Road again?'

'Worse than that Sas. I'm going to leave you with my brother until I return next year.'

'And I thought that we were friends.'

During our travels around New Zealand Sas and I covered a total distance of 11,300 kilometres and the journey took us to sixty randomly selected locations distributed throughout the country. The main objective was to determine if a departure from the tried and tested routes had an alternative travel experience to offer, perhaps one that enabled a different understanding to be gained of the country and it's people. The enforced random selections pushed Sas and I into areas that we did not want to go and challenged us to understand more about the places that we visited. And by taking us to those areas it opened up vistas that very few New Zealanders or visitors will have ever seen and which simply reinforced how very beautiful the country is. From the gorges of Utiku, the sands of Omapere, the views beyond Haketere, the sheer drops around Coonoor, the reflections on the waters of Upokongaro, the curling break of waves on Claris beach, the isolation of Pouto, the rock formations of Oparara. And also the discoveries, the trans-Tasman landing site at Herepo, the poem of Honikiwi, the history of Houhora, the laughter of Algie's Bay, the shoes of Pyramid, the alien landing at Ngatimoti, the pebbles of Quarry Hills, the mystery of Jimmy's Road at Oponae and so on.

And apart from the single location of Gisborne the random selection took us to rural locations where the majority of New Zealanders do not live. They are places whose past is greater than their present, whose contribution to the general wellbeing of the country is largely undervalued, whose futures are in doubt. The church, the community hall, the war memorial, the primary school and the derelict cooperative dairy factory lend a common theme to many of these places. They act as reminders of what New Zealand once was and what it is in the process of rapidly losing. And what it is losing is community.

There is a beauty about New Zealand's rural churches that is unrivalled. It has to do with their wooden construction, their small size, their cleanly painted lines, their white walls, their cool interiors and now silent bells. And the poignant plea of the Nukutawhiti faithful, *'Yes, we are small. And there are those who would get rid of these little churches. Nevertheless, where two or three are gathered together in my name, there am I in the midst of them,'* says it all. The rural churches are dying, just as belief is dying, just as concern for them is dying. In time many will be placed on low loaders and will be transported to desirable suburbs of Auckland, Wellington and Christchurch. John and Jan will invite friends for drinks and they will admire the gleaming kauri and totara flooring whilst the ghosts of the departed and dead will mingle amongst them unnoticed. The church graveyards will no longer be tended and the grass and weeds will grow long and lank until nature finally reclaims all to its own.

The community hall lies unloved and unused. No longer will the hall hold its annual 'stags and hinds' dance to encourage procreation and rural community survival since everyone will be far too busy watching their 'telescreens' or will be communicating online with their three thousand or more virtual 'friends'. The halls were built with great hope by their fathers and forefathers who understood the importance of community. Many of the halls were founded on loss of the most profound kind when the young men of the district left laughing and smiling never to return. How do you describe the grief of parents, siblings, uncles and aunts when the great tragedy of war took so many young men in their prime. It was not as if rural people were unused to death since many years ago childhood had always been a precarious rite of passage. But taking so many young men in so short a time took away the very future of the place. The construction of the memorial halls demonstrated the resilience of the rural people and the respect that they had for the sacrifice of their kith and kin. The halls demonstrated their hope for the future.

The war memorials often sit close to the church, community hall or both. There is a feeling of pride about them, that when called upon we did our bit. It is the surnames which haunt, particularly the two or three of the same name. Dead. The memorials are invariably well tended but the new generation, far removed in time and distance from the wars, wonder about their present day relevance. But sometimes even they must reflect when they see their own surnames engraved in stone. But how long before these memorials join the church and community hall on the road to decay?

Many rural primary schools still sit as a testament to hope, education and progress. In design they are attractive with large windows through which pupils can sit and gaze at the distant landscape where they would far rather be. Perhaps their fathers and forefathers also studied there and maybe that is where their ancestors met their beloved? They are warm, intimate places far distant from their city cousins that have become factories of learning, of experiment, of targets and of disillusion.

For many years New Zealand has been a home for 'lifestyle' properties where people disillusioned with urban life have had the opportunity to become disillusioned with rural life. It doesn't take long for most to realise that you can't make a living from thirty sheep, a few watercolour paintings and a handful of olive trees. That has been the experience of the vast majority of new age life stylers. However this does not mean that a reverse migration to the rural communities is not a good thing. In fact it may be a solution to both the urban and rural malaise. And the critical ingredient for such a movement is broadband access and the internet. Much is written about the power of the internet and how people can work remotely from any location in the world. Indeed many governments subsidise rural internet access and a number of libraries provide access free of charge. Unfortunately this well meaning service is invariably misused and does not fulfil its intended purpose. Youngsters catch up on their Facebook entries and games status whilst others just search out the latest recipes. At the end of the day reliance on government is inefficient and unsustainable and it is up to the rural communities themselves to establish their own cyber enterprises. To achieve that objective they may have to set up their own broadband services and encourage people and businesses with specialist expertise to join their communities. After all it is in their own and their children's interest to stop the current rural decay and resurrect what were once vibrant communities.

What was surprising for such a free and easy going country is the number of private property and no entry signs that have sprung up in recent years throughout the nation. Everyone can respect the right of individuals to have their own privacy, peace and quiet but this current phenomena appears to be part of a national land grab that involves unscrupulous property developers, vested interests and foreign entities who have no interest or understanding of the Kiwi psyche. Some of the most beautiful parts of the country are being sold off to the highest bidder and before long New Zealanders will be tenants in their own land. It is as if an economically beleaguered country is saying to itself *'what else have we got left to sell?'* and what they are selling is the very thing that makes them an independent nation. And once it has gone it has gone for good. And the entities that are buying are not the simple 'buy and sell for a profit get rich quick' capitalists. The entities that are now buying land, mineral resources and forestry are in it for ever and once they have control it is just a resource that they will exploit without any concern for the indigenous people, whether they be 'pakeha' or Maori. They will own them and their children just like medieval serfs.

A visual image that particularly struck Sas and I on our travels was how few people live and work in the rural areas of New Zealand. There is nothing perceptive about this observation since it is characteristic of most developed countries where migration from the land to the industrial cities has taken place for more than three centuries. The difference is that in other countries the contribution of land based industries to the economy is now small, and in many cases insignificant. New Zealand is very different in this respect since agricultural and forestry products represent the most important components of the national economy. Total New Zealand 'merchandise' exports in 2009 were recorded at $39.7 billion whilst service exports, including tourism and consultancy services, were $12.7 billion. The 'merchandise' export figure is particularly relevant since a break down of that figure reveals that the land based industries contribute to eight of the top ten exports namely, milk powder ($4.30 billion), sheep meat ($2.90 billion), frozen beef ($1.56 billion), butter ($1.51 billion), cheese ($1.36 billion), fruit ($1.06 billion), wine ($1.01 billion), and wood ($0.95 billion). The two remaining top ten exports were crude oil ($1.73 billion) and coal ($1.00 billion). The current population of New Zealand is 4.4 million of which the four major cities contribute 53 percent of the total, namely Auckland (1.36 million), Christchurch (0.39 million), Wellington (0.39 million) and Hamilton (0.20 million).

These dry statistics may seem a million miles away from a random journey around New Zealand but in fact they are at the very heart of the matter. The figures indicate that only 14 percent of the population live in the rural areas and yet these people are the major wealth creators of the country. It may seem an unfair point to make but what are the 1.36 million people in Auckland actually doing? How much of the national wealth are they creating? One can only conclude that they are primarily servicing the needs of each other in respect to education, health, social welfare, transport, law and order, consumer goods and so on. If you want to lose an awful lot of friends you might even say that the majority of urban dwellers are living on welfare since they are not actually creating new wealth.

In a democracy, and thank goodness for that, every adult has a vote. Parliaments are of relatively short duration and therefore the individual political parties cater for the needs of their individual electorates and in New Zealand, as in most developed countries, they are in the main urban in nature. And so by this measure the rural areas that we visited no longer have any voice and will never have any voice. Perhaps all countries are on the same self-destructive downward spiral where powerful political and business interests continually dictate that the nation needs more people to create demand for yet more houses, cars and consumer goods. Instead the policy is rapidly taking every nation into the realms of the lunatic asylum. What countries should aspire to is a stable educated population that can use modern technology to create more wealth for the individual and the country as a whole. If any country can break this cycle it is New Zealand. Can it do so? Yes. Will it do so? Most probably not.

The random journey confirmed one thing in my mind and that is that New Zealand is the most beautiful country in the world. Others may dispute this point of view and that is perfectly understandable, but I would be very happy to argue the case. New Zealand is a great little country as are the people that inhabit it. Long may it remain so.

Millennium Monument, Napier.

Map of Randomly Selected Locations, New Zealand.

About the Author

Trevor Cree was born in Steyning, Sussex, and has lived there most of his life. He studied agricultural engineering at the University of Newcastle upon Tyne and spent his professional career working in over 30 countries worldwide undertaking short-term consultancy assignments for various international entities, including the UN Food and Agriculture Organization (FAO), European Union (EU) and UN High Commissioner for Refugees (UNHCR). Travel to countries such as China, North Korea, Sudan, Yemen, Iraq, Iran, Syria, Moldova, Albania, Liberia and Sierra Leone influenced his views on the importance of democracy and democratic accountability. From 2012 onwards he took an active part in parish council affairs in Steyning in an effort to increase openness and transparency in local government.

'Random Journeys: New Zealand', originally published in 2011, was the result of a long-term love affair with New Zealand and its people.

Books by the same Author

Track (2005)

Random Journeys - New Zealand (2011)

Modbury Tales (2022)

The Writer's Diary (2022)

The Clock Tower Affair (2025)

Printed in Dunstable, United Kingdom